HIGH-PERFORMANCE
BICYCLING
NUTRITION

Richard Rafoth M.D.

BICYCLE BOOKS

FROM

MBI Publishing Company

First published in 1998 by MBI Publishing Company, 729 Prospect Avenue, PO Box 1, Osceola, WI 54020 USA

MBI Publishing Company books are also available at discounts in bulk quantity for industrial or sales-promotional use. For details write to Special Sales Manager at Motorbooks International Publishers & Wholesalers, 729 Prospect Avenue, PO Box 1, Osceola, WI 54020 USA.

Library of Congress Cataloging-in-Publication Data

Rafoth, Richard.
    High-performance bicycling nutrition / Richard J. Rafoth.
       p. cm.
    Includes index.
    ISBN 0-933201-92-3 (pbk. : alk. paper)
      1. Cyclists--Nutrition. I. Title
TX361.C94R35 1998
613.2'024'7966--dc21   98-22666

On the front cover: Fresh fruit is a key component to the high-carbohydrate, low-fat diet necessary for training and competition. The triathlete on the cover is selecting fruit at a stand in the San Francisco Bay area. *Nick Cedar*

Printed in the United States of America.

Contents

Introduction

Our athletic abilities are a reflection of our inherited or genetic potential and our level of training or conditioning. But reaching a personal "best" also requires proper nutrition and hydration. This book will explain the basics of athletic nutrition to help you maximize your personal potential.

We can't change inherited traits such as lung capacity, muscle fiber composition, body type, or the mechanical advantages of limb and muscle length. However, we can control our physical and nutritional training programs, maximizing the benefits of conditioning and avoiding the harmful effects of poor nutrition.

Our genetic makeup not only sets an upper limit for our performance but also influences how quickly we can train up to that level. As a rule, no two bicyclists on the same training regimen will improve at the same rate. A study of 650 bicyclists participating in a two-week training program confirmed this variability with a 4-percent performance improvement at the low end and up to a 40-percent improvement for those who progressed rapidly. How can we use this information to tailor our own personal training programs? Here are six tips:

1. **Be Persistent.** Even though your peak performance may be genetically predetermined, a cyclist who trains consistently will prevail over a genetically gifted slacker.
2. **Be Patient.** Some of us reach our maximum more slowly. In fact, one study clearly documented changes in muscle fibers continuing throughout a five-year training program!
3. **Vary Training Routines.** When you feel you may have reached a plateau, try something different, such as intervals or weight training.
4. **Ride Smart.** Technique (e.g., smooth pedal stroke), tactics, and psychological toughness are important attributes of a premier rider. Smart riders focus on more than just aerobic or anaerobic capacity. And a positive attitude can make a big difference.
5. **Set the Right Goals.** Set realistic goals that give you the satisfaction of achievement, rather than the disappointment of failing at the impossible. Breaking that "PR" (personal record) can often mean more than winning a criterium.
6. **Eat Right.** And don't neglect the role of a well-thought-out nutrition program. It won't substitute for a good physical training program, but good nutrition will play a key role in maximizing your athletic performance.

CHAPTER ONE

The Physiology of Digestion

A side from being a pleasant diversion for the bicyclist, food is a necessity in providing the energy you need to move you and your bike. In this opening section, we will discuss the principles of digestion, absorption, and metabolism in converting food energy into a form that can be used by the muscle cells. We'll also look at the components of food and how they fit into the process.

We'll be getting into some technical terms and tables, but as you read on, this information will make more sense, and you'll be able to use it to plan your nutrition program. Understanding how food is digested will give you perspective on the energy conversion process and will ultimately help you become a better and more efficient bicycle rider.

The Raw Materials

Let's start with a look at the basic components of food. All foods are composed of carbohydrates, fats, and protein. Carbohydrates are the primary energy source for bicyclists of all abilities, as well as other athletes involved in short, maximum performance events. Fats offer an alternative energy source and are more important for slower endurance events. Proteins are used to maintain and repair cells and tissue throughout the body. They are used as an energy source only in situations of severe malnutrition.

Some foods provide more energy per portion than others as the energy content of equal weights of carbohydrate, fat, and protein is not the same. Energy content is expressed in Calories (Cal) in the American system of units or kilojoules (kJ) in the international, or scientific, system of units (see Appendix B for an explanation and the relevant conversion factors).

The energy in one nutritional Calorie (note the uppercase "C") is the equivalent of a kilocalorie, i.e., 1,000 calories (lowercase "c"), or 4.18 kilojoules. Carbohydrates and protein each contain four Calories of energy per gram while a gram of fat at nine Calories per gram has more than twice the energy content. The customary abbreviations and measurement conversions for the various units discussed here are listed in figure 1.1 on the following page.

Fig. 1.1. Calorie/kilojoule Abbreviations and Conversion Table

Calorie =	Cal =	4.18 kJ
kilocalorie =	kcal =	4.18 kJ
calorie =	cal =	4.18 J
joule =	J =	0.24 cal
kilojoule =	kJ =	1,000 J

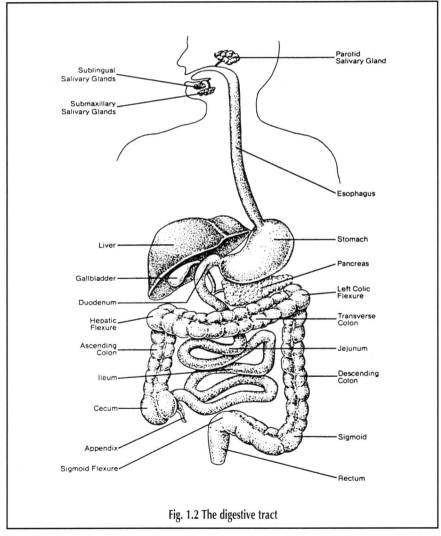

Fig. 1.2 The digestive tract

Digestion

Understanding digestion, the first step in converting food energy into the energy of muscle action, is critical to the bicyclist. The mechanical and chemical changes begin in the mouth, continue in the stomach, and are completed in the small intestine, where absorption takes place. Figure 1.2 represents the digestive tract and will be helpful as a reference.

The initial step in the digestive process is mechanically breaking down large food particles to allow digestive enzymes to reach individual food molecules and begin the chemical changes needed for absorption. This mechanical action begins with chewing, continues with the muscular churning of the stomach, and is completed as this semi-liquid material known as chyme is moved through the small intestine.

The chemical processing of individual food molecules begins when digestive enzymes are secreted into the chyme by cells in the stomach, pancreas, and small intestine. Only then can absorption take place.

When designing a nutritional program for athletes, the speed at which digestion and absorption takes place is a key concern. The time needed for food to travel from the mouth, through the stomach, and into the small intestine, where the food molecules will be absorbed into the bloodstream, affects how quickly food energy will be available to the muscle cells for exercise.

Four important factors which influence the speed of the digestive process are:
1. the form of food (solid or liquid)
2. the fat content
3. the sugar concentration
4. the level of physical activity

Liquids are emptied from the stomach more quickly than solids. Although chewing helps, it is the initial form of the food—liquid versus solid—that is most important. Studies have shown that it takes up to 4 hours for a solid meal to be mechanically altered and emptied from the stomach, while 75 percent of a meal that is already in liquid form empties into the small intestine within an hour. The volume of fluid in the stomach also plays a role; keeping the stomach filled speeds the rate of gastric emptying.

Fat slows emptying of the stomach. Solid foods with moderate fat content empty more slowly than lean or non-fatty ones. Fatty liquids empty more slowly than those that are fat-free. However, a liquid with some fat will still empty more quickly than a low-fat, solid food which must first be mechanically altered by the stomach.

THE PHYSIOLOGY OF DIGESTION

Fluids with a high sugar content also delay stomach emptying. When a concentrated sugar solution enters the small intestine, it will actually draw water from the body before absorption will take place. To protect against rapid fluid shifts, there is a reflex slowing of stomach emptying. The concentration of sugar molecules in a solution is referred to as its osmotic activity—the higher the concentration of molecules, the higher the osmotic activity. And the greater the discrepancy between the osmotic activity of the solution and the osmotic activity of the body fluids, the greater the effect to slow stomach emptying. (If the osmotic activity of the drink is equal to that of body fluids it is referred to as isotonic, and if it is higher than body fluids it is hypertonic.)

Any delay in stomach emptying is a particular problem for the competitive athlete who is trying to balance the needs of maximizing energy intake with concentrated sugar solutions, avoiding volumes of unneeded fluids while minimizing the effects of too high a concentration which delays delivery to the site of absorption in the small intestine. The answer lies in the use of complex carbohydrate drinks.

Osmotic activity (and concentration) is directly related to the number of individual molecules of sugar per defined volume of fluid usually water. If several molecules of sugar (glucose) are physically linked, the result is a single molecule of complex carbohydrate which now contains the energy equivalent of the several original glucose molecules but affects the (osmotic activity) as a single molecule. By using complex carbohydrates, more molecules of glucose energy can be delivered into the small intestine in a small volume of water than by using simple glucose solutions.

Vigorous physical activity also slows the mechanical activity of the digestive tract. A fast walk (with a heart rate of 108 beats per minute) slowed stomach emptying and intestinal absorption by almost 40 percent in one study. In another study, when exercise increased beyond 70 percent of a person's maximum physical capacity (VO2max), stomach emptying progressively slowed until all digestive tract muscular activity ceased. Fortunately, cycling does not usually require this level of exertion except in certain competitive events.

Once you understand the four factors that affect stomach emptying, you can make sound nutritional decisions based on the type of ride you are planning and the urgency of your Calorie needs. When a quick energy boost is needed during a ride, a carbohydrate drink is ideal. The endurance rider, on the other hand, might prefer a carbohydrate energy bar which will empty from the stomach more slowly and be absorbed over a longer period of time. And a small amount of fat will prolong the digestive and absorptive process even further, provide extra Calories, and improve the taste.

Carbohydrates

Carbohydrates are the major dietary energy source for most adults. They contain four Calories of energy per gram, and provide between 40 and 60 percent of the daily replacement Calories in the average American diet. During exercise, carbohydrates are even more important as a fuel source. An understanding of their absorption and metabolism is essential in developing a program to maximize performance.

During digestion, carbohydrates are broken down into single molecule units, absorbed, and circulated to the cells via the blood. Any excess carbohydrate not immediately used by the cell is stored in the liver and muscles as glycogen, a complex carbohydrate of glucose molecules.

The basic building blocks of all carbohydrates are single sugar molecules, or monosaccharides. They deliver energy to the body quickly because they do not need to be digested further before absorption takes place. Glucose and fructose are the two most common monosaccharides in our diet. The linking of two monosaccharides results in a disaccharide, while long chains of sugar molecules are referred to as complex carbohydrates, or polysaccharides.

Most dietary carbohydrate is in the form of one of two disaccharides (sucrose and lactose) or complex carbohydrates. Sucrose is found in familiar table, or cane, sugar and also in apples, bananas, and oranges. Lactose is the milk sugar in dairy products. Complex carbohydrates, or starches, are primarily supplied by grains.

Before they can be absorbed from the intestinal tract, all disaccharides and complex carbohydrates are first converted to the monosaccharide, or single molecule, form. Digestion of complex carbohydrates begins in the stomach, where salivary enzymes, mixed with food during chewing, convert up to 40 percent of dietary starch into disaccharide form. The remainder is broken down in the upper small intestine by pancreatic enzymes. The final step in this process, the reduction from disaccharide to monosaccharide form, is the result of enzymes secreted by the lining cells of the small intestine.

For many years it was believed that glucose-containing carbohydrate drinks with a concentration of 2.5 percent (weight of glucose per weight of water) were the maximum tolerated without nausea and a delay in stomach emptying. But more recent studies have demonstrated normal emptying with concentrations up to 8 percent, and nausea occurred only when concentrations were pushed above 11 percent.

Interestingly, the old standbys such as apple juice and cola drinks have a sugar concentration of 10 percent. Although glucose polymer sports drinks will provide more Calories per quart at the same overall sugar molecule (osmotic) concentration, there is no performance advantage in taking your Calories as complex carbohydrates. But the absence of the sweet taste and nauseating properties often found in the high-concentration, pure sugar drinks is a definite plus for sports drinks in maintaining a steady glucose energy intake during the ride.

After monosaccharides are absorbed by the small intestine, they are transported throughout the body via the circulatory system. They are then moved into muscle and liver cells where they are either metabolized immediately to release energy, stored as glycogen, or converted to triglycerides (fat). Liver and muscle cells are the major storage sites for glycogen. The average 160-pound person has approximately 365 grams of carbohydrate stored as:

liver glycogen: 110 grams
muscle glycogen: 245 grams
extracellular blood sugar: 10 grams

During training and competitive events, the body draws heavily from liver and muscle glycogen for its energy supply. These 365 grams contain almost 1,500 Calories of energy, which will fuel several hours of cycling at a brisk pace or 1 hour of out-and-out racing. As these internal glycogen reserves fall, there is an increasing dependence on the glucose absorbed from snacks and drinks.

Movement of glucose out of the bloodstream and into the cell is controlled by the hormone insulin which is produced by specialized cells in the pancreas. Insulin, released in response to a rise in the blood glucose level from intestinal absorption, increases the movement of glucose into the body's cells, preventing an excessive rise in the blood sugar level. Glucose is then used to meet the cell's energy requirements, stored as glycogen, or converted into fat. Although some glucose can enter the cell without insulin, the transfer rate increases 25 times when insulin is present.

Vigorous physical exercise will increase the movement of glucose into muscle cells, independent of insulin, by increasing the permeability of the cell membrane to glucose. As a result, blood insulin levels can drop to 50 percent of their resting level during exercise.

Understanding this relationship between food absorption, insulin release, and glucose uptake by the cells is important when planning pre-event nutrition for bicyclists and other athletes. A sugary drink, for example, will be quickly emptied from the stomach and absorbed in the small intestine. The blood sugar then rises and insulin is released by the pancreatic cells. Glucose moves into the body's cells. But the insulin effect may persist after all the sugar in the drink has been absorbed from the intestine. If additional sugar or carbohydrate is not eaten, the blood sugar can then drop below a critical level (referred to as hypoglycemia), resulting in weakness and poor athletic performance. To prevent this "reactive" hypoglycemia, the bicyclist should avoid all rapidly absorbed, sugary foods (especially liquids) for several hours immediately before exercise. Solid foods (which are emptied from the stomach and absorbed more slowly) containing carbohydrate are much less of a problem.

During exercise, on the other hand, any glucose absorbed from the intestine will quickly move into the cells without insulin, blunting the rise in blood sugar. Additional insulin release from the pancreas is limited, and a drop of the blood sugar to hypoglycemic levels is much less likely.

Besides their role as an energy source, sugars may affect our mood. There is some evidence that eating sugary foods stimulates the internal production of endorphins, opiate-like hormones also stimulated by exercise. And the insulin released in response to a rise in blood sugar has been linked to an increase in the levels of brain serotonin, a chemical compound which has a calming effect.

Are there negative effects as a result of eating sugar? Tooth decay is a proven hazard. And for those with a more sedentary lifestyle, swings in the blood sugar level may promote the growth of body fat stores, stimulate the appetite, and increase food cravings.

Fats

Fats provide from 20 percent to 40 percent of the Calories in an average American diet. More than 90 percent of these Calories are in the form of triglycerides, which are fat molecules made up from a single glycerol molecule and three fatty (FA) molecules. The rest of the fat Calories in an average diet are in the form of cholesterol and phospholipids.

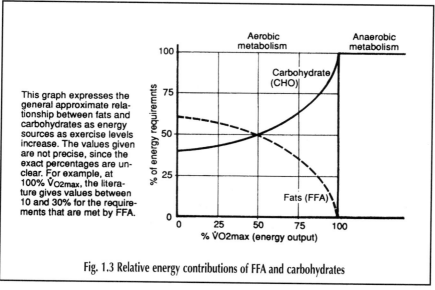

This graph expresses the general approximate relationship between fats and carbohydrates as energy sources as exercise levels increase. The values given are not precise, since the exact percentages are unclear. For example, at 100% V̇O2max, the literature gives values between 10 and 30% for the requirements that are met by FFA.

Fig. 1.3 Relative energy contributions of FFA and carbohydrates

THE PHYSIOLOGY OF DIGESTION

While cholesterol and phospholipids are building blocks for cell growth, triglycerides are metabolized for their energy content. They are most important in endurance activity where they provide more than 50 percent of the muscle energy at lower activity levels (less than 50 percent VO2max). They are less important in maximum performance events such as sprints (90 to 100 percent VO2max), which are fueled primarily by energy from carbohydrates.

Fatty acids also provide certain essential building blocks for the cellular machinery. They cannot be synthesized or produced by the cells themselves and must be included in the diet. It has been estimated that these essential requirements would be met by a diet containing only 15 to 25 grams of fat, which is about 10 percent of our total daily caloric needs. Additional fat Calories are used purely for their energy value.

Essentially all fat digestion occurs in the small intestine, with bile from the liver aiding enzymes from the pancreas. The individual fatty acid molecules are cleaved from their glycerol backbone to become free fatty acids (FFA). The free fatty acids are then absorbed from the small intestine, moved into the lymph system, and ultimately emptied into the circulatory system. They are then distributed throughout the body and into the cells where they are metabolized as an immediate energy source, or reconstituted into triglycerides for storage, mainly in fat cells.

As energy demands increase, the reverse process occurs. Triglycerides stored in fat cells are broken down and individual FFAs are transported to the muscle cells, where they are metabolized. Fats are the main energy source for the muscle cell after cellular glycogen stores have been depleted.

There are four types of dietary fat: saturated, monosaturated, polyunsaturated, and trans fats. A discussion of each would prove useful for the bicycle athlete.

Saturated Fat

Saturated fat, generally from animal fats such as meat, cheese, and dairy products, is hard at room temperature and is the least desirable, from a health perspective. Saturated fat increases the level of low-density cholesterol (LDL, the bad one) and is a major factor in the development of clogged arteries, strokes, and heart attacks.

Monosaturated fats

Monosaturated fats are from vegetable oils, such as olive, canola, and peanut oils and are liquid at room temperature. They actually have a slight cholesterol-lowering effect when overall fat intake is low (less than 60 grams per day). They don't affect the level of either LDL or of high-density lipoprotein (HDL), which can actually help your arteries by carrying cholesterol out of your tissues.

Polyunsaturated fats

Polyunsaturated fats, also found in plant oils such as soybean, cottonseed, corn, sunflower, and safflower, contain essential fatty acids needed for cell growth and repair. As they increase the level of HDL and reduce the level of LDL, they are the least harmful to the blood vessels of all dietary fats . (Note that not all plant oils are polyunsaturated. Some, such as coconut, palm, and cocoa butter are highly saturated.)

Trans fat

Trans fats are formed when unsaturated fats are artificially hydrogenated, a process in which hydrogen molecules are added. Trans fats were developed to meet the public demand for unsaturated fats which were not greasy or oily. Unfortunately, hydrogenation creates a fat which is metabolized as a saturated fat, raising the level of LDL. In fact, trans fats may be worse than monosaturated fats because they not only raise the LDL, but also lower the level of HDL . . . a double whammy.

Is there a good fat? As a rule of thumb, polyunsaturated fats are preferred for a normal diet. Trans fats, which are found in a multitude of processed foods (referred to as "Partially hydrogenated vegetable oils" on the label) should be avoided whenever possible. Check the label carefully; a product labeled, "Contains no cholesterol," may still contain trans fats.

Other tips to help you avoid the really bad trans fats include:
1. Checking your margarine to be sure it contains only liquid vegetable oil
2. Experimenting with vegetable oil instead of margarine in your cooking
3. Using canola or olive oil when you stir fry

There have been a flurry of recent articles and books touting the advantages of a high-fat diet in improving competitive aerobic performance. These diets contain at least 30 percent fat Calories, 30 percent protein Calories, and only 40 percent carbohydrate Calories. At this time there is no proof that a high-fat diet improves high-level aerobic performance when compared to an equal-caloric high carbohydrate diet which is relatively fat-restricted with less than 20 to 25 percent total Calories as fat It has been suggested that any improvement is a placebo effect from the improved taste of foods containing a higher percentage of fat.

Two well-controlled studies have looked at the effect of a high-fat diet in improving endurance performance. A high-fat diet (70 percent fat in one study, 38 percent in the other) did increase the time that elapsed before exhaustion for exercise performed at the relatively moderate rate of 50 percent VO2max. The results were 80 versus 42 minutes of cycling in one study and 76 versus 70 minutes of running in the other. Glycogen-sparing effects were studied to determine if there was a preferential shift to fat metabolism during exercise, but none were found.

A third study tracked Calorie replacement after exercise. Two groups were studied: one on a low-fat diet and the other eating normal, high-fat foods. The study found that those on a low-fat diet did not replace the Calories spent during their training program, while those on a more liberal fat diet did. This suggests that poorer performance on a low-fat training diet might result from a cumulative caloric deficit, which would result in more limited glycogen stores at the start of the event, rather than any advantage of fat over carbohydrates as a muscle energy source.

Decades of research and clinical studies have documented the negative effects of a high-fat diet on health, including its role in hypertension, atherosclerosis, heart disease, and certain cancers. To help lower these risks, most health authorities recommend a diet that is low in fats, high in carbohydrates, and rich in fruits, vegetables, and whole grains. However, there are limits to these reductions because fat is important to the texture and taste appeal of food.

Protein

Protein is the third major food component, making up 20 percent of our daily caloric intake. It provides the building blocks to repair cell injuries, including the microtrauma (microscopic injury to the muscle tissue) that occurs with exercise. It is only rarely used by the body as an energy source.

The building blocks of proteins are the single-molecule amino acids. Protein digestion begins in the stomach with enzymes secreted by the stomach lining cells and is completed in the small intestine by enzymes from the pancreas and small intestinal cells. The free amino acids are then absorbed by the small intestinal lining cells, transported by the blood, and removed by individual body cells.

Of the 20 amino acids needed for cell growth and survival, 11 can be synthesized within the cells of the human body and are referred to as nonessential amino acids. The other nine, which are essential to cell survival, must be provided by the diet. Both meat and vegetables are good sources of protein, but animal proteins contain a better balance of essential and nonessential amino acids. Vegetarians must eat a larger variety of foods to assure that their amino acid requirements are met, being careful that these proteins "complement" each other to supply all the essential amino acids.

Each individual cell has an upper limit for protein storage. After this limit is reached, excess amino acids are converted into triglycerides or glycogen. In other words, a high-protein intake will not automatically force additional muscle (cell) formation, but is instead converted into fat. Studies of trained athletes have proven that

1.2 grams of protein per kg (kilogram) of body weight per day are adequate for the muscle development required in most sports. Even in strength training, protein in excess of 2 grams per kg per day will be metabolized into fat. Active athletes on a balanced diet that replaces their daily Calories will almost always get adequate protein for tissue growth and repair. Even in extreme endurance activities such as the Tour De France, daily protein requirements were easily satisfied by the normal (unsupplemented) diet.

The average 70-kg (154-pound) cyclist needs 70 to 100 grams of protein per day. Lean beef, skinless chicken, and fish will provide 7 grams of protein per ounce, cooked beans provide 6 grams per half cup, and other cereal grains such as rice provide about 3 grams per half-cup serving. A cup of milk or yogurt supplies 8 grams of protein. So it's relatively easy to satisfy your daily protein requirements with 6-8 ounces of meat, 2–3 servings of dairy products, and 6–10 servings of cereal per day.

Detailed studies have shown that protein provides less than 5 percent of the energy expended during exercise, and only during starvation or extreme malnutrition will protein be used as a primary source of energy for cell function. Numerous studies of diet supplements have failed to support any advantage of a high-protein training diet for high-level aerobic performance. And one study actually demonstrated a decrease in overall performance from the appetite-suppressing effects of protein foods, which led to a decrease in carbohydrate intake and diminished muscle glycogen stores.

Effects of Exercise on Digestion

Occasionally cyclists will develop gastrointestinal (GI) complaints during training and competition. These symptoms, usually from the lower intestinal tract or colon, are much more common in runners and triathletes than in bicyclists. In a recent survey of triathletes in a half iron man event, 50 percent complained of belching and flatulence. Most symptoms occurred during the running portion of the competition.

Blood flow to the digestive tract is reduced during vigorous exercise, with reductions of up to 80 percent after 1 hour of bicycling at 70 percent VO2max. And those bicyclists with the most severe symptoms demonstrate the greatest decrease in blood flows. Mechanical trauma from the movement of the small and large intestines within the abdominal cavity may explain why runners have more problems than bicyclists or swimmers. Changes in GI hormone levels have also been measured with vigorous exercise, but a cause-and-effect relationship to symptoms has not been proven. Stress is also important as a factor in such pre-competition symptoms as nausea, vomiting, and diarrhea.

THE PHYSIOLOGY OF DIGESTION

Heartburn, or esophageal reflux, more frequently occurs as a result of exercising immediately after eating. The increase in reflux is related to a delay in stomach emptying with exercise and the increased volume of food and acid in the stomach that is available to reflux. An increase in reflux also results from the physical jostling that occurs in sports activities, especially in running. Heartburn is usually a minor problem for cyclists and is best handled by delaying exercise for several hours after a meal or using antacids or one of the over-the-counter, acid-reducing medications, such as Tagamet or Zantac.

Exercise does delay stomach emptying, and the more vigorous the exercise, the greater the delay. Running, again, has a proportionately greater effect compared to bicycling or swimming. In addition to increasing esophageal reflux, and slowing the absorption of any Calories eaten, the delay in stomach emptying may lead to a sensation of fullness and nausea. Eating a high-fat or high-protein meal and using hypertonic drinks appears to compound the problem. Forty percent of triathletes using a hypertonic sports drink had severe complaints, when compared to only 11 percent of those who had used isotonic drinks.

Finally, the bicyclist should note that exercise does increase the frequency of defecation. Although it has been speculated that changes in digestive hormones associated with exercise might stimulate the colon, it is more likely that the mechanical factor of jostling the bowel is again the culprit. A fiber-rich training diet also plays a role. In one survey, triathletes who experienced cramps had all eaten a high-fiber, pre-competition meal, while only 10 percent of those without cramps had done so.

The effects of exercise on the digestive tract are more problematic for runners, and thus triathletes, than for bicyclists. And except for competitive bicyclists, the effects of exercise on the GI tract are rarely a problem. If heartburn or bloating is a problem, a 3- to 4-hour fasting period before your ride may be helpful. While on the bike, eat small, frequent snacks and avoid hypertonic sports drinks, especially if you're doing a vigorous workout. And stay hydrated. If you're dehydrated, the stomach will empty even more slowly, and the decrease in blood flow to the digestive tract will be accentuated. Finally, although some racers will eat a low-residue diet for several days before an event to minimize cramps and the frequency of bowel movements, this greatly complicates diet planning. For the rest of us, slowing the pace will usually decrease the urge until a bathroom is located.

CHAPTER TWO

The Physiology of Energy Production

M aximizing muscle energy output is important to bicyclists at all skill levels. It will be very helpful to understand how proper nutrition can produce the energy needed to achieve personal cycling goals. In this chapter, we'll take a look at the processes that produce muscle energy from food.

As we noted in the previous chapter, all foods are composed of carbohydrates, fats, and protein. Carbohydrates are the primary source of muscle energy for the average bicyclist or other athletes involved in short, maximum performance events. Fats also serve as an energy source, particularly for endurance events performed at a slower pace. Proteins are used to maintain and repair body tissues, and are only rarely used to supply energy to the muscles.

Food energy is released through a chemical reaction with oxygen in a process called oxidation. When oxidation occurs outside the body—for example, when oil (a fat) is burned in a lamp or when a flaming sugar cube (a carbohydrate) is used as a decoration in a dessert—this energy is released as heat and light. In the body, however, food energy needs to be released more slowly into a form that can be harnessed for basic cell functioning and transformed into physical activity by the muscle cells. This is accomplished by transforming carbohydrates and fats into a single common chemical compound known as adenosine triphosphate (ATP), which will harness and transfer the energy from the food molecules into muscle action.

ATP contains ribose (a sugar), adenosine, and three phosphate groups. The chemical bonds in the phosphate groups contain the energy in the molecule, and it is the breaking of these bonds that powers muscle contractions. The cell has a limited capacity to store ATP, and with exercise the muscle cell ATP is depleted within seconds. To sustain activity, the body must continually resynthesize ATP through one of three pathways: phosphocreatine metabolism, anaerobic glycolysis, and aerobic glycolysis.

Let's review the role of these three pathways in powering muscle activity. When a nerve impulse first arrives at the muscle cell, stored ATP is used to contract the resting muscle. When stored ATP has been depleted (a short burst of muscle activity of several seconds at most), phosphocreatine is metabolized to resynthesize ATP and continue physical activity for another 5 to 10 seconds before its stores have been exhausted. As you might guess, it is most important in sprint activities lasting up to 10 seconds.

After phosphocreatine reserves have been exhausted, anaerobic glycolysis, the second pathway, utilizes the energy from carbohydrate metabolism to continue to resynthesize ATP. This pathway does not require oxygen, but a build-up of lactic acid begins within minutes, producing physical discomfort and affecting exercise performance by limiting muscle cell contraction. Anaerobic glycolysis is useful for short bursts of activity lasting several minutes at most. It cannot supply the ATP needed for longer, endurance activities.

The third pathway, aerobic glycolysis, is oxygen dependent. The breakdown of phosphocreatine and anaerobic glycolysis will support the regeneration of ATP while the respiratory and heart rate increase to ensure adequate oxygen delivery to the cell, at which time the aerobic pathway takes over to meet the majority of the cell energy requirements. The anaerobic pathway will continue to function at a low level producing lactic acid as one of its products of metabolism. These limited amounts of lactic acid are quickly metabolized by the liver and muscle cells and do not accumulate to any degree.

The aerobic pathway is used preferentially as the muscles' energy source, as long as adequate oxygen is being delivered to the muscle cell. Energy needs can outstrip the availability of oxygen to support the aerobic pathway in, for example, a sprint. Then, stored ATP, the phosphocreatine system, and anaerobic metabolism will all help to supply the additional short-term energy needs. Later, when the activity level returns to a level sustainable by the aerobic system, ATP and phosphocreatine regenerate themselves. At the same time, the liver and muscle cells clear the excess lactic acid produced during the sprint. With conditioning, the body will accommodate higher and longer levels of activity, using only the aerobic pathway. The body will also recover more quickly from the effects of an anaerobic sprint.

The oxygen dependent, or aerobic, metabolic pathway is very efficient, with almost 40 percent of the energy contained in the glucose molecule being available to the cell for muscular activity via ATP. The remainder is lost as heat. Oxygen-independent, or anaerobic, metabolism is much less efficient, with only 2 percent of the glucose energy being converted into muscle activity.

The Cardiovascular System

Aerobic energy production at the cell level is dependent on energy stores (glycogen and fat) in the muscle cells, and adequate oxygen from the cardiovascular system (heart and blood vessels). With training there is an increase in the amount of blood pumped through the muscle capillaries per minute (cardiac output) as well as an increase in the aerobic metabolic enzymes in the skeletal muscles. But the increase in cardiac output is the more important of the two changes. Since the maximum heart rate is lower following exercise training, this increase in the cardiac output is due to a higher stroke volume (amount of blood pumped per heart beat).

Oxygen Consumption

There are two commonly used measures of energy metabolism—VO2 and lactate threshold (LT).

Oxygen consumption, the total volume of oxygen utilized by an exercising individual per minute, is referred to as VO2. And VO2max is the maximum amount of oxygen that the lungs and cardiovascular system can supply to exercising muscle cells. When oxygen requirements of the task at hand exceed an individual's VO2max, anaerobic energy pathways take over.

The more strenuous a physical activity, the higher the volume of oxygen (VO2) utilized for energy production. And your reserve can be estimated by comparing the VO2 for the specific activity to your own VO2max, expressing the ratio as a percentage of the maximum possible. Moderate activity is usually considered as VO2 at 50 percent VO2max, while activity above 80 percent VO2max is quite strenuous.

VO2 is proportional to your heart rate—remember that oxygen is transported by the cardiovascular system and heart rate reflects the amount of blood pumped per minute. And at 60 to 70 percent of your maximum heart rate, you are exercising at 50 to 85 percent of your VO2max. So for most training calculations, you can measure your pulse rate, calculate its percent of your maximum heart rate, and assume that is the percent of VO2max for that activity.

The blood lactate threshold (LT) reflects our level of conditioning. The LT is the percentage of VO2max at which lactic acid from anaerobic metabolism begins to accumulate in the blood. An individual's LT improves with training. In other words, the percent VO2max, or percent maximum heart rate at which blood lactate levels begin to rise, will increase. This reflects an improved efficiency of the aerobic energy systems and an increase in exercise efficiency. Because aerobic metabolism is so much more efficient than anaerobic metabolism, an individual with a high LT uses less of their glycogen fuel for any given level of muscle activity. As a result, they can exercise longer at that level of exertion before their muscle glycogen stores are depleted.

THE PHYSIOLOGY OF ENERGY PRODUCTION

The Muscle

Now it is time to look at the "engine" that converts food energy to mechanical performance: the muscle. Learning a little about how the muscles work should be of particular interest to the bicyclist who relies so much on them.

As with any other engine, the efficiency of the human muscle is measured as the percentage of energy input converted to actual mechanical work. Under optimal conditions, the muscle converts 20 to 25 percent of the chemical energy available in the foods we eat into physical performance. The rest is released as heat.

Skeletal muscle makes up over half of the body weight in a lean individual. These muscle cells contain two proteins—actin and myosin—which chemically interact to shorten the muscle cell when stimulated by nerve impulses. This process requires energy provided by ATP.

There are two types of muscle fibers: Type I, or slow twitch, and Type II, or fast twitch. The slow-twitch muscle fibers are more efficient, using both fats and carbohydrate for energy. They are the major muscle fiber in use at 70–80 percent of VO2max. Fast-twitch fibers, on the other hand, are less efficient, using mainly glycogen as fuel. They are called into action for sprints as the athlete approaches 100 percent of maximum performance.

The carbohydrates and fats used as fuel by the muscle cell are available from reserves within the cell itself. They are also available as fuel by way of the bloodstream from intestinal absorption as glucose and free fatty acids, or mobilization from storage in liver cells and fatty (adipose) tissue. Muscle cells contain a significant proportion of the body's glycogen stores but a relatively small amount of triglycerides. Muscle glycogen and triglycerides offer the advantage of being immediately accessible as an energy source without the intermediate step of transportation by the circulatory system.

Muscle Energy Supply and Fatigue

Although carbohydrates supply the majority of the energy for muscles during vigorous activity, fats provide more than 50 percent of the Calories used during moderate exercise (less than 50 percent VO2max) even when adequate muscle carbohydrates are available. As exercise increases toward 100 percent VO2max, the proportion of the total energy Calories supplied by fats diminishes. And in sprint events, where metabolism becomes anaerobic (greater than 100 percent VO2max), fat metabolism ceases to be a significant factor in supplying energy to the muscle. Some athletes have been interested in using dietary fat, both in the training diet and

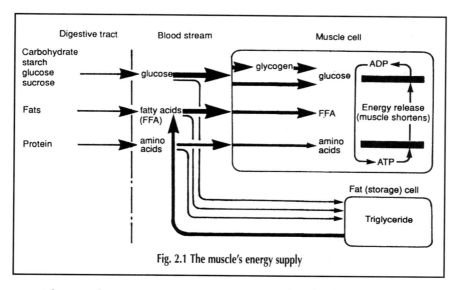

Fig. 2.1 The muscle's energy supply

as supplements during competitive events, to manipulate this fat/carbohydrate ratio in supplying energy to the working muscle, and thus improve athletic performance. Although there is some evidence that fats may help prolong endurance activities at less than 50–60 percent VO2max, there is no proven benefit of fats for high-performance activities (90–100 percent VO2max).

When muscle glycogen has been depleted, the muscle is dependent entirely on fats for its energy supply. However, as fat is less efficient as an energy source than carbohydrate, a work level above 50–60 percent VO2max cannot be maintained. Initially, the liver supplements muscle carbohydrate needs during sustained exercise by releasing glucose into the circulation to maintain a stable blood sugar level. The "bonk" or "hitting the wall" occurs when liver glycogen is finally depleted and energy output is completely fat-dependent and limited to 50–60 percent VO2max. It would be logical to assume that if adequate carbohydrates (to offset those expended) were replaced by oral supplements during a ride, the cyclist could maintain his or her pace indefinitely. Unfortunately, this is not the case. Studies have shown that cyclists with low muscle glycogen stores, but high blood glucose levels, still experienced fatigue, even though the onset of that fatigue was delayed by ingesting carbohydrate supplements. Unknown factors, perhaps related to physical changes in the muscle cell itself, are thought to be responsible. This type of fatigue is more common in the untrained athlete. At exhaustion, irreversible changes occur in the muscle cell itself, and further competitive activity is impossible, no matter what the blood sugar level.

THE PHYSIOLOGY OF ENERGY PRODUCTION

Muscle cells oxidize the carbohydrate glucose, and other sugars must first be converted to glucose by the liver before they can be used as fuel by the muscle. Although they may be more palatable, numerous studies have failed to demonstrate any performance advantage to glucose polymers, fructose, or sucrose (common table sugar which is a disaccharide of glucose and fructose) for carbohydrate replacement as compared to glucose alone assuming similar concentrations and normal stomach emptying.

Now, let's look at the contributions of glucose and fats to muscle energy needs relating to the phase of exercise. During prolonged aerobic performance (greater than 50 percent VO2max but less than the 100 percent of maximum performance), three distinct phases of exercise have been identified.

In the first phase, which occurs during the first few minutes of exercise before increased muscle blood flow and other cellular adaptations to exercise have occurred, glycogen is the primary source of muscle energy. As much as 20 percent of the total muscle glycogen stores may be consumed during this phase.

During the second phase, there is a shift in energy metabolism to a mixture of carbohydrate and FFA. Muscle glycogen stores continue to decrease, reflecting their ongoing utilization, but now the muscles also extract and metabolize FFA and glucose from the arterial blood supply. During moderate exercise, FFA and carbohydrates contribute equally as an energy source. At lesser intensities the ratio changes, with FFA taking on increasing importance. And as exercise increases and the anaerobic threshold is approached at 100 percent VO2max, the opposite shift occurs, with almost all muscle cell energy supplied by carbohydrate alone.

The third phase starts when muscle glycogen is completely depleted. It is at this point that a sense of fatigue occurs, exercise intensity cannot be maintained, and muscle metabolism shifts almost entirely to FFA.

In the well-fed and rested state, the human body contains approximately 1,500 carbohydrate Calories stored as glycogen in the liver and muscle, and over 100,000 Calories of energy stored as fat. This is adequate carbohydrate for several hours of brisk bicycling, and enough fat to support cycling at a reduced level (50–60 percent VO2max) for days.

Let's review four practical points for the bicyclist.

First, there is adequate liver and muscle glycogen to support 1 to 2 hours of bicycling at 70 percent VO2max. A good training program and riding at a reasonable pace to take advantage of fat Calories for energy will postpone the time at which glycogen is finally depleted and fatigue occurs.

Second, a good oral intake of carbohydrates to supplement muscle and liver stores will help to maintain an adequate blood sugar level and extend internal carbohydrate stores for events expected to last more than 2 hours. It is best to begin the carbohydrate supplements at the start of the event, as they are much less effective after the bonk has occurred. A well-trained cyclist will need slightly more than one gram of carbohydrate per minute to sustain maximum performance. Oral supplements should aim to replace carbohydrate at that rate.

In addition to extending the time to reach fatigue during longer, moderate-activity events, one recent study has suggested that maximal performance in a 1-hour, high-intensity time trial (80 percent VO2max) can also be improved with oral carbohydrate supplements. Drinking 1 liter of a 7-percent carbohydrate solution at the start and during the ride improved times by 2 percent.

Third, even with optimal nutrition, a point is ultimately reached where exhaustion occurs and the rider has to slow down or stop.

Finally, even though greater amounts of glycogen in the cell can prolong the duration of any bicycling activity, they cannot increase the muscle's maximum energy output.

Muscle Pain and Cramps

There are three types of muscle pain related to exercise: muscle pain or discomfort, muscle soreness, and muscle cramps. Let's review each.

Muscle pain or discomfort

Exercise that requires significant effort, either from high-energy demands (low resistance, rapid contraction rate) or substantial muscle effort (high resistance, low contraction rate) is often associated with muscle pain or discomfort. No study has identified a single cause for this discomfort, although the fact that it occurs more quickly in a muscle with a limited blood supply suggests that the culprit is a product of muscle metabolism. In addition, the fact that the ingestion of sodium bicarbonate will delay the onset of this pain indicates the culprit is acidic in character. Lactic acid is considered the likeliest candidate, although other metabolites such as pyruvic acid and ammonia have also been suggested.

Muscle soreness

Delayed-onset muscle soreness begins 24 to 48 hours after exercise and peaks in 48 to 72 hours. It is most evident after muscle activity such as raising or lowering a weight which actively resists lengthening of the muscle, and places tension on muscle fibers and connective tissue. This is in contrast to isometric muscle activity where there is very little shortening of the muscles but greater increase in the tone of muscle fibers. It is related to muscle damage (most likely minute tears and physical damage) rather than the build-up of metabolic byproducts during exercise. Muscle biopsies conducted in research situations have demonstrated muscle contractile fiber damage and an inflammatory response.

Muscle cramps

Muscle cramps are an indication that you have used your muscles beyond their training limits, either as a result of longer than normal duration or at a higher than normal level of activity. This explains why cramps are more common at the end of a long or particularly strenuous ride, or after a particularly vigorous sprint. In a study of bicyclists competing in a 100-mile race, 70 percent of male participants experienced cramps. Women, interestingly, had a rate less than half as frequent at 30 percent.

Although cramps may be the result of fluid and electrolyte imbalance from sweating, individuals involved in activities requiring chronic use of a muscle without sweating (musicians for example) will also experience cramps. As with the two types of muscle pain, training will decrease the possibility of cramps for any level of activity.

A sports drink may be of help, but it is likely that any benefit is from maintaining hydration, rather than from the small amount of electrolytes they contain. And water is still a lot less expensive.

Conditioning

Conditioning or training will increase maximum muscle energy output (important for short events such as sprints) as well as increase the muscle's efficiency for any given level of exertion. The latter is important in improving results for longer-duration events. Training effects are specific for the muscle groups being exercised; that is, they are activity- or sport-specific. But there is also an effect on the cardiovascular system which benefits all aerobic activities.

Improvements in performance are the result of:

1. an increase in the number and size of muscle mitochondria
2. an increase in the activity of metabolic enzymes in the muscle cell
3. an increase in the number of capillaries that supply blood to the muscle
4. an increase in cardiac output

Although some of these changes begin within days of starting a training program, and most positive effects are seen within a few months, training will continue to produce improvements over many years. One study suggested that conversion of Type II to the more efficient Type I muscle fibers continued throughout five years of regular exercise.

Athletic performance is the ultimate yardstick of training improvement, but the effects of conditioning can be measured in several other ways. The percentage of Calories derived from fat metabolism at any given activity level or percentage of VO2max is increased (Fig. 1.3). This promotes glycogen sparing and increases the duration of activity to exhaustion for any level of exertion.

VO2max is increased, which means that at maximal or near maximal levels of athletic performance, more energy will be supplied from efficient aerobic metabolism than from inefficient anaerobic metabolism.

And finally, there is a shift in the blood lactate threshold (LT) so that less lactic acid accumulates for any level of energy output. This reflects a decrease in production—a shift toward more efficient aerobic glucose metabolism—and a more rapid clearance of the lactic acid produced. As lactic acid has a negative effect on muscle contractile proteins, this shift in the LT minimizes deterioration in muscle performance.

As a result of these training changes in metabolism, an individual can exercise at any given level of activity (percent VO2max) for a longer time before muscle glycogen stores are depleted and the bonk occurs. And if a sprint is needed at the end of the ride or race, the better-trained rider or competitor increases their odds of having the muscle glycogen to fuel a successful effort.

CHAPTER THREE

The Energy Requirements of Bicycling

As we plan our training diet, an understanding of the energy needs for bicycling is equally as important as appreciating the advantages and disadvantages of the various foods that will fuel our human machine. As you review the energy requirements of bicycling, you will see references to both Calories (with a capital "C") and calories (with a lowercase "c"), which quantify the energy content of foods, the energy released by cellular metabolism, and the energy expended by physical work performed.

In physical science (physics and chemistry), a calorie (with a lowercase "c") is defined as the amount of energy required to raise the temperature of one gram of water one degree centigrade. In discussions of human energy metabolism, this unit is too small to easily express the energy expended in biologic systems. So, the Calorie (with a capital "C"), which is equivalent to 1,000 calories or one kilocalorie, is used instead. Nutritionists often forget the capital "C" when they are writing about calories (which should really be Calories), so don't get confused.

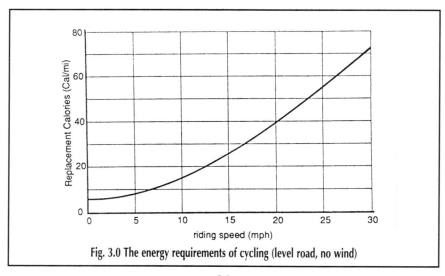

Fig. 3.0 The energy requirements of cycling (level road, no wind)

In the previous chapter, we learned that ATP, or adenosine triphosphate, is the common energy carrier to transfer the energy in foodstuffs to the cells. As this energy transfer takes place, large portions are lost as heat. On the average, about 60 percent of all the energy in the food we eat produces heat during the process of ATP formation. Additional energy is lost, again as heat, when energy transfer takes place from ATP to muscle contraction. As a result, only 25 percent of the energy contained in the food we eat actually produces mechanical work.

On the other hand, the bicycle is a very efficient machine. More than 95 percent of the bicyclist's energy is translated into forward motion and less than 5 percent is lost as heat, due to the resistance of the bearings, rolling resistance of the tires, and other factors.

When bicycling on a flat route, overcoming the resistance of the air molecules to the movement of the bicyclist consumes the majority of our energy output. Our air speed, the speed at which we are moving against these molecules, is not necessarily the same as the speed being recorded on our bicycling computer (our ground speed). On a windless day, air speed and ground speed are exactly the same, but in a head wind, our air speed will be greater than our ground speed, and our energy needs per mile will be increased. A tail wind will decrease our air speed in relation to our ground speed, and our energy expenditure per mile will go down as well. Accurately calculating energy needs requires an understanding of this relationship.

This relationship between energy expended and air speed is an "exponential" one, which means that doubling our air speed more than doubles the energy needs per mile. This relationship is illustrated in figure 3.1. On hilly terrain, additional energy is required to lift the bike and rider against gravity. The exact calculations are covered in appendix A. As a point of reference, the energy expended per mile of bicycling is about one-fifth that of running.

Friction

Friction, or the resistance to the moving parts of the bicycle itself, is unavoidable in bicycling, but it can be minimized. Minimizing friction provides a performance edge in short, competitive events and will significantly decrease the energy needs on longer rides.

If bearings and chain are well lubricated and adjusted, they will absorb only 3 to 5 percent of the rider's energy output . The resistance of wheel and bottom bracket bearings can be further reduced for special events, such as time trials and pursuits, if the grease is removed and replaced with a light oil. However, they must be oiled frequently; oil, unlike a coating of grease, does not give protection from moisture and dirt. The bicycle chain should be well-worn and lubricated with a light oil. Heavier lubricants, such as paraffin, last longer but increase friction.

THE ENERGY REQUIREMENTS OF BICYCLING

As the tire rolls, the compression and expansion of the tread, casing, and sidewall are the factors contributing to the rolling resistance of your bicycle. Rolling resistance is also directly related to the size of the tire "footprint," or contact patch where the tire physically meets the road. Rolling resistance can be decreased by using a higher inflation pressure and using thinner, more flexible tires. You can usually judge the quality of a tire by pinching the casing to test its pliability. Light, thinner-walled tires and tubes are almost always better. Natural latex is more elastic than synthetic butyl rubber. Extra layers of material, belts, and liners will cause more friction.

Weight

The weight of the rider and the bike need to be considered in determining cycling energy requirements. First, the energy required to move a bicycle and rider over a flat course, with speed remaining constant, is directly related to the total weight of the rider and bike.

The same is true when bicycling up a hill, which is why a heavier rider usually climbs more slowly. But the heavier bike and rider have the advantage in being able to descend more quickly than a lighter one. The downhill speed is a result of the propulsive forces (total rider/bike weight and the angle of the hill) and the resistive forces (frontal surface area of the bicyclist moving against the resistance of the air molecules). The weight of the rider is more important than wind resistance, with the heavier rider having the advantage going downhill. Although a heavier rider can descend faster than a lighter one, the time gained fails to make up for time lost while climbing. This explains why lighter riders have a natural advantage on hilly rides. But big riders should not despair; conditioning and riding technique can offset this climbing advantage of lighter-weight riders.

Weight is also a factor in accelerating or rapidly increasing the speed of the bike. It takes more energy to accelerate a heavier rider/bike combination in a sprint. And the extra weight of moving parts on the bicycle (wheel rims, for example) may require twice as much energy to accelerate in a sprint as an equal amount of weight in the frame. If you're on a limited budget, upgrade your tires, rims, crankset, and bike shoes before you buy that new frame.

And we often forget the weight we carry: the extra water bottle, the larger and heavier tool set, and even that extra pancake we ate in the morning. Dropping a few ounces here will have as much impact on our performance as that expensive titanium item you've been saving to buy.

Air Resistance and Drafting

Remember that the speed used to calculate energy expenditure is your air speed and not the ground speed shown on your computer. So if there is a head wind, add that speed to your ground speed to determine your air speed and amount of air resistance. And if there is a tail wind, subtract it from your ground speed. If you think about it, this makes sense; it is always easier to ride with a tail wind.

At 20 miles per hour, two-thirds of our energy output is used to overcome air resistance alone. For example, when speed is increased from 7.5 miles per hour to 20 miles per hour, mechanical resistance increases by 225 percent, rolling resistance by 363 percent, and air resistance by 1,800 percent. This explains the energy-saving or performance advantage of drafting and using aerodynamic equipment. A recent study nicely demonstrated that at 20 miles per hour, drafting a single rider reduced energy requirements (measured as VO2) by 18 percent and at 25 miles per hour by 27 percent. Using aerodynamic rims with 16 to 18 spokes gave a 7-percent benefit at 25 miles per hour, which surprisingly bettered the 4-percent advantage of a set of disc wheels and equaled the benefit of a specially designed aerodynamic bicycle.

Wind tunnel results have demonstrated that eliminating 10 grams of drag will save 158 feet in a 25-mile time trial. How much is 10 grams? It's the drag created by projecting 4.5 inches of a pencil into the airstream. That baggy jersey or upright position may be costing you minutes.

Cross-Training

A popular myth is that one can cross-train for aerobic events. For example, the belief is that a runner who bicycles in the summer could resume running in the fall with little change in performance. While the concept of cross-training is valid for the recreational athlete attempting to maintain a general level of cardiovascular conditioning, it is not an option for the competitive athlete. Many of the benefits of conditioning are specific for the muscle groups being used. Studies of triathletes, for example, have consistently demonstrated that bicycling does not improve running performance; running only slightly improves bicycling performance; and swimming has no effect whatsoever on the other two events.

Cycling and Weight Control

There is an epidemic of obesity in countries such as the United States and those in western Europe where over one-third of adults are overweight. Although genetics play a role, our genes have been the same for thousands of years; only recently has obesity dramatically increased. It appears that reduced physical activity, rather than increased food intake, is the major culprit. And the difference is about 300 Calories a day, which could be offset by an hour of easy bicycling.

Physical activity has a positive effect on your weight and figure by:
1. increasing energy output and caloric expenditure
2. suppressing appetite

29

THE ENERGY REQUIREMENTS OF BICYCLING

3. increasing Basal Metabolic Rate (BMR)
4. maintaining lean body mass at the expense of fat

The basic premise of all weight-control programs is that weight loss occurs when the number of Calories expended, or burned, over a 24-hour period is greater than the number consumed. The net deficit is covered by Calories from the fat reserves, and this results in weight loss. One pound of body fat equals 3,500 Calories.

Bicycling will increase your daily caloric output in two ways. First, and most obvious, is through the energy required to move you and your bicycle against the resistance of air and gravity. A second, more indirect effect is through subtle changes in your daily routine to include more physical activity, such as walking up a flight of stairs instead of taking the elevator. This sort of activity works to give you an increased sense of vigor and well-being.

Many dieters worry that increased physical activity will increase their appetite. However, a recent carefully controlled study of overweight individuals did not reveal a proportionate increase in appetite with exercise. This lends support to the positive role of physical activity in reaching the goal of a negative caloric balance and resulting weight loss. In fact, vigorous exercise actually suppressed appetite for several hours. By planning your exercise immediately prior to your major meal of the day, this short-term effect can be used as an effective appetite control strategy.

Competitive athletes will often lose weight no matter how many Calories they attempt to eat. As might be expected, this weight loss results when the Calories expended are more than the number replaced. This is most pronounced in competitive swimmers. As a group, they train long hours, are unable to eat while swimming, and have too few waking hours left to replace those Calories, which can be as many as 7,000 Calories with only 6 or 7 nonexercise waking hours. This is less of a problem for bicyclists who can eat while riding.

Regular exercise also increases your basal metabolism rate, or BMR (the number of Calories utilized by the body at rest to maintain basic life processes). An increased BMR is associated with all aerobic conditioning activity and is maintained with as little as 30 to 40 minutes of exercise, four times a week. One study indicated that the increase in BMR with regular exercise may be even more pronounced in the older athlete.

Not only is there an increase in your daily BMR with regular exercise, there is also an additional post-exercise boost that burns an additional 15 Calories for every 100 Calories used during your aerobic activity. To capitalize on this post-exercise bonus, consider two or more rides per day—perhaps in the morning and after work—rather than a single ride of equal duration.

Regular physical exercise will also protect muscle mass (at the expense of fat) during periods of negative Calorie balance and weight loss. If you study two groups, one active and one more sedentary, with an equal weight loss, the exercise group will lose less muscle mass.

Does exercise lead to selective fat loss in the exercised limbs? Can fat be taken off the thighs by bicycling? Unfortunately, this doesn't happen. As an example, comparing the fat fold thickness in the left and right arms of professional tennis players does not demonstrate a difference or asymmetry. While exercise will promote the loss of total body fat, this loss cannot be targeted to any specific body area. But improving the muscle tone in the exercised limb or abdominal muscles has the same apparent effect.

Are there any shortcuts to weight loss? Some authors have suggested that riding at slow speeds (less than 50 percent VO2max) is preferred in a weight-loss program, as more of the Calories expended will be supplied from fat tissue at these lower levels of exercise. Let's look at this argument in more detail. If you ride at 65 percent VO2max, your body's fat stores will provide about half of your caloric needs; the other half come from glycogen reserves. At 85 percent VO2max, the relative number of Calories supplied from fat fall to about one-third of the total expended with the balance, again, coming from glycogen reserves. However, if one looks at the absolute numbers, a fit bicyclist riding 30 minutes at 65 percent VO2max will burn about 220 Calories (110 fat Calories, 110 Calories from carbohydrate or glycogen stores). The same bicyclist, riding at 85 percent VO2max, will burn an additional 100 Calories (a total of 320 Calories over the 30 minutes), with 110 Calories still coming from fat and 220 from carbohydrates. The actual number of fat Calories burned during the 30 minutes of exercise remains unchanged.

It is the final balance between total Calories expended from any source, carbohydrate or fat, and those eaten (the net caloric balance) that determines whether weight is gained or lost. One advantage of riding more slowly is that it makes the ride a more enjoyable experience for the novice rider, and the pace can be maintained for hours. But if you have only a limited amount of time to ride, the faster your average speed, the more Calories burned . . . and the more weight you will shed. If your goal is losing weight, the bottom line is to ride at a pace that is comfortable for you, push yourself occasionally for the cardiovascular benefits, and avoid replacing more Calories than you expend.

At one time there was speculation that if you exercised at a slow pace, minimizing the use of muscle glycogen Calories, and then ate carbohydrates post-ride, the very fact that there were still glycogen reserves in the muscle would divert these carbohydrate Calories into fat. This is unproved.

The Zone by Barry Sears takes a unique approach to weight loss. He claims that a relatively high-fat diet (40 percent carbohydrates, 30 percent protein, 30 percent fat, compared to the currently recommended athlete's diet of 60 percent/15 percent/25 percent, respectively) not only improves athletic performance but also promotes weight loss. However, most sports trainers remain skeptical, and years of nutritional research fail to support him on either point.

According to his theory, too much carbohydrate intake facilitates obesity by stimulating the pancreas to release excessive amounts of insulin. He speculates that with time, the fat cells become resistant to these higher levels of insulin, leading to a vicious cycle of even more insulin release. He suggests that these high-insulin levels promote additional fat synthesis. His argument seems to be flawed, as it puts the cart before the horse. It is obesity, not high carbohydrate intake, that leads to insulin resistance at the cell level and results in overproduction of insulin by the pancreas. Support for the latter is found in the fact that losing weight, even while maintaining a high carbohydrate intake, restores insulin sensitivity at the cell level.

And as to the weight-loss advantages of a high-fat diet, a recent Cornell University study of volunteers on two ad lib (eat as much as you want) diet regimens (either high, with 37 percent fat or low, with 22 percent fat) for 11 weeks demonstrated that those on a low-fat diet ate fewer total Calories and lost twice the weight of those on the higher-fat diet.

Four Practical Tips for Weight Control

1. **Dieting Alone Doesn't Help.** You will lose weight, but it will be more than fat. Some is muscle (which actually burns Calories for you!!) and can leave you thinner, but also slower and weaker. And with less total muscle mass, a return to prediet eating patterns can actually lead to more rapid weight gain and stabilization at a higher level than where you started.

2. **Ride Regularly.** This will help to maintain your muscle mass while you are shedding fat. And even at a recreational pace of 15 miles per hour, 1 hour a day of riding will burn almost 4,000 Calories per week (the equivalent of a pound of fat) above and beyond your normal activities.

3. **Eat a High-Carbohydrate Diet.** The diet that is best for endurance performance (60 to 70 percent carbohydrate, low in fat) is also the best for weight loss.

4. **Add Weight Training.** As riding uses mainly lower-body muscles, weight training will help to protect the upper body during this time of negative caloric balance. A program of 20 to 30 minutes, three times a week is enough to maintain muscle mass, and the increased muscle tone and positive feeling that go with it are a big plus to keep you on track toward your weight-loss goal.

Although the bottom line of any cycling weight-control program will be read from the bathroom scale, you can make a rough estimate of your weight loss using the information in figures 3.1 and 3.2.

Figure 3.1 Caloric Expenditure When Cycling

Riding Speed		Calories Expended			
mph	**km/h**	**Cal/mi**	**Cal/km**	**Cal/hr**	**Cal/min**
5	8.0	7.4	4.6	87	1.5
6	9.6	8.3	5.2	100	1.7
7	11.2	9.3	5.8	115	1.9
8	12.8	10.5	6.6	134	2.2
9	14.4	11.9	7.4	157	2.6
10	16.0	13.4	8.4	184	3.1
11	17.6	15.1	9.4	216	3.6
12	19.2	16.9	10.6	253	4.2
13	20.8	18.9	11.8	296	4.9
14	22.4	21.1	13.2	345	5.7
15	24.0	23.4	14.6	401	6.7
16	25.6	25.8	16.2	463	7.7
17	27.2	28.5	17.8	534	8.9
18	28.8	31.3	19.5	613	10.2
19	30.4	34.2	21.4	700	11.7
20	32.0	37.3	23.3	797	13.3
21	33.6	40.6	25.4	903	15.0
22	35.2	44.0	27.5	1019	17.0
23	36.7	47.6	29.8	1146	19.1
24	38.4	51.4	32.1	1283	21.4
25	40.0	55.3	34.6	1433	23.9
26	41.6	59.4	37.1	1594	26.6
27	43.2	63.6	39.8	1767	29.5
28	44.8	68.0	42.5	1954	32.6
29	46.4	72.5	45.3	2154	35.9
30	48.0	77.2	48.2	2356	39.4

Values are based on the following assumptions:
1. 75-kg rider with 10-kg bike
2. 25-percent efficiency of converting food Calories into muscle energy Calories
3. Estimated basal metabolism of 50 Cal/hr

THE ENERGY REQUIREMENTS OF BICYCLING

Figure 3.2 Bicycling and Weight Control

Calorie intake per 24 hrs (C_i) _____Cal

Basal metabolic rate per 24 hrs (C_b) _____Cal
wt in lbs x .45 x 24

Calories expended by cycling (C_e) _____Cal
figure 3.1

Adjustment for BMR in
 figure 3.1 (C_a) _____Cal
hrs of exercise x 50 Cal/hr

Net Calorie gain (loss) per 24
 hours (C_n) _____Cal
C_i-C_b-C_e+C_a

Weight Gain (loss) in lbs
 per 24 hrs _____lbs
C_n/3,500 Cal/lb

CHAPTER FOUR

The Basics of Athletic Nutrition

Now that we have covered the basics of digestion and the energy require-ments of cycling, let's use this knowledge to develop a practical nutrition program to maximize your performance and enjoyment of the sport. Let's take a minute to review some of the key points to be considered in the process.

Carbohydrates (fruits, vegetables, and grains) are the primary energy source for our daily activities and are the only energy source for high-level aerobic perform-ance. Adequate dietary carbohydrates will spare fats and cellular proteins that would otherwise be broken down and metabolized for their energy content. Simple car-bohydrates (refined sugars) can provide a rapid burst of energy, but overwhelming evidence supports the performance advantage of complex carbohydrates (starches) which are absorbed more slowly, require less insulin for their metabolism, and, as a result, produce a more even and constant blood sugar level.

Fats are an energy source for slower, endurance activities and provide certain essential building blocks for the cellular machinery. It has been estimated that these essential requirements would be met with a diet containing only 15 to 25 grams of fat, or about 10 percent of our total daily caloric needs, while any additional fat Calories are either used for their immediate energy value or stored for future use. There is no proof that eating a high-fat diet improves maximum aerobic perform-ance above that of an equal caloric diet minimizing fat. It has been suggested that any improvement is probably a placebo effect from the sense of well-being associ-ated with eating foods containing a higher percentage of fat.

Protein provides the basic building blocks for cell growth and repair. Only in severely malnourished individuals will protein be used as an energy source. Additional dietary protein requirements for the muscle development stimulated by conditioning are quite small compared to our normal daily protein intake. There is no evidence that a high-protein diet will speed up or force this muscle development, or improve athletic performance in any way. In fact, there is some evidence to the contrary, as a routinely high-protein diet may be harmful to the kidneys.

Carbohydrates are the optimum energy food for all athletic activities. They are easily digested and absorbed, and are also the most readily metabo-lized to ATP. Fats have the disadvantage of slowing gastric emptying and absorption, while proteins have a very complex metabolism that limits their availability as an energy source.

THE BASICS OF ATHLETIC NUTRITION

During exercise, certain carbohydrates are used preferentially to meet the energy needs of the muscle cell. The carbohydrate stored in the muscle fibers as glycogen is used first. Once muscle glycogen has been depleted, blood glucose provides the carbohydrate energy for the exercising muscle. As blood glucose (blood sugar) is used by the muscle cell, it is replaced either by glycogen stored in the liver or carbohydrates eaten and absorbed from the digestive tract. Oral supplements will delay the use and depletion of our liver glycogen stores. When the liver glycogen finally is depleted, the muscle cell is entirely dependent on glucose absorbed from the digestive tract or fat metabolism to meet its energy needs. If there is no glucose available, hypoglycemia and fatigue occur. This is the "bonk" or "hitting the wall" that bicyclists are familiar with.

In chapter 1 we reviewed four factors that influence the digestive process and shorten the time to provide that supplemental blood glucose: the form of the food (liquid is better), the fat content (lower is better), the sugar concentration (optimum concentration of 7 to 10 percent), and the level of physical activity (more vigorous activity delays absorption).

Psychological Effects of Foods

Psychological factors play a major role in competitive cycling, and addressing them plays a role in most training programs. The foods we eat can affect our mood and attitude. Standardized psychological profiles revealed an increase in depression scores in trained athletes when the training diet failed to replace the training Calories expended. This is considered a normal response to the chronic fatigue which occurs with chronic caloric deficiency, particularly in competitive performers who expect the best from themselves at all times.

Nutrition also has an impact on anxiety and arousal levels. Supplements of vitamins B1, B6, and B12 have been reported to lessen anxiety in pistol shooting and may have some applicability to bicycling events requiring high concentration. And a part of caffeine's positive effect on performance may be through an effect on arousal. Finally, branched-chain amino acids have been reported to modify central fatigue mechanisms, but benefits for athletic performance are unproved at this time.

But most important of all may be a placebo effect from the feeling of well-being that follows a meal or a favorite food.

Four Phases of Athletic Nutrition

When discussing a nutritional training program for any athletic event, it is helpful to think in terms of four phases. Each phase plays a distinct role in enhancing performance and is approached differently. The *Training Diet* lays the groundwork for the event ahead, by meeting the nutritional requirements of the physical training program during the days and weeks before the ride. The *Pre-ride Interval* refers to the hours immediately preceding the ride and "tops off the tank" with glycogen fuel to support upcoming energy needs. The diet during the pre-ride interval, as well as the nutritional supplements during the *Ride* itself, are a key to achieving that extra performance edge. The *Post-event Recovery Period* begins the preparation for the next ride. These four phases can be remembered as the "Four 4s to reach your personal best": the 4 days prior to the event, the 4-hour pre-ride interval, the 4 minutes immediately before the ride and the ride itself, and the 4-hour post-event recovery period.

Training Diet

The body's glycogen stores (365 grams, 1,500 Calories) on a normal diet will support several hours of recreational cycling before muscle glycogen depletion and fatigue occur. Although these normal stores are adequate for the average bicycle commuter, a quick training ride, or for competitive events lasting less than 1 hour, the endurance rider or racer participating in longer events will benefit from pre-exercise carbohydrate loading to maximize these muscle glycogen reserves.

Muscle glycogen content varies with the carbohydrate content of our diet. After three days of a high-carbohydrate diet (70 percent of the total dietary Calories as carbohydrate), total muscle glycogen stores are significantly higher than on the standard American diet (50 percent of Calories as carbohydrate). Increasing the amount of stored glycogen will increase the length of exercise until fatigue, but will not increase our maximum performance (VO2max) during that time.

The classic carbohydrate loading program starts six days prior to the anticipated competitive event. On Days One through Three, a vigorous workout of 1 to 2 hours duration is used to deplete muscle glycogen. The athlete also stays on a low-carbohydrate diet (no more than 10 percent of total Calories from carbohydrates) to maximize the exercise depletion effects. This is followed by three days (Days Four to Six) of a carbohydrate-rich diet with only light exercise to maintain muscle flexibility. For these final three days, the bicyclist should have at least 600 grams of carbohydrate per 24 hours, with the last carbohydrates being eaten 4 to 6 hours prior to the event. This program first depletes all muscle glycogen and then takes advantage of a rebound effect that actually overloads the muscle with glycogen during the period of high carbohydrate consumption. This results in muscle glycogen levels 50 percent higher than on a standard diet.

A high-carbohydrate diet alone (without the preceding three-day carbohydrate depletion phase) will provide 90 percent of the benefits of the full six-day program, avoiding the digestive turmoil that carbohydrate depletion and loading can produce. Other disadvantages of carbohydrate loading include the difficulty of maintaining the initial low-carbohydrate diet, problems with weight gain during the high-carbohydrate and low-exercise portion of the program, and complaints of muscle heaviness and stiffness thought to result from the excess glycogen and associated water present in the muscle fibers.

The amount of water retention is significant. There are three grams of water stored in the muscle for each gram of carbohydrate. This translates into a 2- to 7-pound weight gain from water alone. Water retention can have a positive performance effect with the water released as glycogen is metabolized, decreasing fluid replacement needs. There are occasional EKG (cardiac) changes due to glycogen loading of the heart muscle, but long-term harmful effects have not been substantiated.

Even though muscle glycogen is highest after the six-day program, it is not clear that there is a performance improvement over a three-day, high-carbohydrate diet alone. Considering the potential problems, most athletic trainers are currently recommending three days of high-carbohydrate intake immediately prior to the event, eliminating the depletion phase.

Is there an optimum training diet for the bicyclist? There is overwhelming evidence that dietary carbohydrates are the key to maximum performance. We know that a chronic caloric deficit will lead to progressive muscle glycogen depletion and fatigue. We also know that you will replace almost 100 percent of your depleted muscle glycogen on a diet that includes 10 grams of carbohydrate per kilogram of body weight per day. But it is not clear that increasing carbohydrate intake above 3,000 Calories per day will produce any additional improvement in performance, assuming that your total daily Calories replace those used for your training program.

If you are interested in multi-day endurance events, there may be an advantage in increasing your fat intake to 30 percent of total Calories for the several weeks prior to the event. But there is no evidence that a high-fat diet improves single-day, high-performance (greater than 60 percent VO2max) activities, and there are definite long-term health questions about high-fat diets. As total caloric needs increase with training or riding, a high-fat diet (more than 20 percent of total caloric needs) might be considered as a way to maintain a positive caloric balance if carbohydrates alone are not meeting the challenge.

And finally, there is no evidence that more than one gram (or at most 1.5 grams) per kilogram body weight per day of protein is beneficial in endurance, sprint, or power performance.

Figure 4.1 Training Diet Worksheet

I. Determine caloric needs

BMR (wt in lbs x .45 x 24)	_____	Cal
+ energy expended cycling (figure 3.1)	_____	Cal
TOTAL (A)	_____	Cal

II. Diet composition

Calculate BW in kg

BW = 0.455 x wt in lbs (B) _____ Kg BW

Protein

1.5 grams protein/kg BW x B _____ gm protein/24 hrs (C)

Fat

minimum of 25 grams per day up to
average U.S. diet of 70 gms per day _____ gm fat/24 hrs (D)

Carbohydrate

Total caloric needs (A)	_____	Cal
Protein Cal = C x 4.1 (E)	_____	Cal
Fat Cal = D x 9.3 (F)	_____	Cal
Carb Cal = A - E - F	_____	Cal carb/24 hrs (G)
Grams carb/24 hrs = G/4.1	_____	gm carb/24 hrs

I. Calculation of daily caloric needs.

II. Determination of specific protein, fat, and carbohydrate needs. Protein based on average daily needs. Fat based to some degree on bicyclist's tastes. Carbohydrates calculated to make up caloric difference to meet needs as determined in I.

Avoid any major changes in diet during the three- or four-day, pre-competition period. The above suggestions need to be customized for your own digestive and metabolic functions. Any advantage of carbohydrate loading, or shifting the make-up of your diet, can be more than offset by the GI (gastrointestinal) distress or indigestion brought on by new foods or food combinations. As in all things, moderation is important.

A balanced diet with an emphasis on carbohydrates appears to offer the maximum benefits during this period. Figure 4.1 may help you in planning your training diet.

Pre-exercise Diet

There is universal agreement on the importance of the pre-race meal. While it takes one to three days to maximize muscle glycogen, liver glycogen levels can change in hours.

THE BASICS OF ATHLETIC NUTRITION

The pre-race meal will top off these liver stores. And a recent study, demonstrating a 15 percent increase in endurance performance with a 300-gram carbohydrate meal eaten 4 hours before exercise, credited improvement to prolonged digestion and continued glucose absorption, supplementing muscle and liver glycogen stores, well into the exercise period.

Sugary drinks should be limited during this 4-hour period. The insulin surge that accompanies carbohydrate absorption increases the potential for hypoglycemia to occur with poor performance as a result. During exercise, this rise in blood sugar from intestinal absorption (and insulin surge as a response) is blunted as exercise facilitates the movement of blood sugar into the cell.

As nervousness will delay gastric emptying, fasting for the 3 to 4 hours before the event will help to minimize the risk of stomach distention and discomfort.

The ideal strategy for the pre-exercise period is to eat a low-fat, non-liquid, 300-gram complex carbohydrate meal 4 hours before the event, avoid sugary liquids during the four hours immediateley prior to exercising, snack on a 45-gram confectionery bar high in simple and complex carbohydrates 5 minutes before the event, and begin liquid carbohydrate supplements with the start of the ride.

Exercise

Early in the exercise period, almost all the glucose fuel for the muscle cells comes from muscle glycogen. As muscle glycogen is steadily depleted, the percentage of carbohydrate energy supplied via blood glucose steadily increases until it reaches 100 percent in the third and fourth hour. The blood sugar level is maintained by the breakdown and release of liver glycogen, glucose absorbed from oral intake, and glucose synthesized in the liver via gluconeogenesis, which is glucose formed as an intermediate step in fat and protein metabolism.

This relationship between muscle, liver, and blood carbohydrates explains the performance-enhancing effect of oral carbohydrate snacks for exercise lasting more than 1 hour. In fact, one study suggested that after only 1 hour of exercise, blood sugar was already supplying 75 to 90 percent of the carbohydrate needed for metabolism by the muscles. Maximizing liquid carbohydrate replacement while riding is a very important strategy for events lasting more than 2 hours. Starting oral carbohydrate supplements early in the ride will conserve muscle and liver glycogen, delaying the time at which complete depletion and fatigue occurs. One to two grams of carbohydrate per minute can be absorbed to sustain prolonged exercise. For example, starting an event with 400 milliliters of an 18 percent glucose polymer solution in the stomach and drinking 100 milliliters every 10 minutes will deliver 108 grams of carbohydrate in 600 milliliters of fluid every hour.

In extreme events such as the Tour de France, for example, by using 20 percent carbohydrate solutions and drinking 2 to 4 quarts an hour, the competitors were able to replace 50 percent of their daily energy expenditure while on the bike.

Carbonation does not affect the emptying rate of the stomach. Three independent studies found no difference in the gastric emptying rates of water, carbonated water, and carbonated carbohydrate drinks. Carbonated colas, which contain 160 Calories per 12-ounce can and the caffeine equivalent of half a cup of coffee, remain a favorite drink of many cyclists.

Free fatty acids (FFAs) also supply energy for the actively exercising muscle. The fact that fat metabolism provides a greater percentage of the total energy Calories at lower levels of activity (50 percent VO2max) presents us another option to protect the muscle's glycogen reserves. Indeed, "going out fast" (more than 70 percent VO2max) is inefficient, as far as glycogen use, with almost all energy Calories coming from muscle and liver glycogen. The prudent cyclist will cycle at 50 to 70 percent VO2max, sparing both muscle and liver glycogen by increasing the energy Calories from FFA metabolism.

The specific sugar, either glucose or fructose, does not appear to be a factor in performance, but the form of the supplement does. A study comparing equal caloric feedings of liquid and solid carbohydrates showed that the riders eating the solid carbohydrates were able to sustain a longer sprint until exhaustion at the end of the ride, although maximum pace, heart rate, and total energy expenditure were the same in both groups. It was speculated that this resulted from the sustained release of glucose energy into the blood stream from the solid carbohydrate, due to the additional time required for digestion and absorption. Solid carbohydrates would appear to be preferable early in the ride, with a liquid glucose drink providing a quick energy boost after all glycogen reserves have been exhausted.

Glucose polymers, which are complex molecules made up of several individual glucose molecules, have been marketed both as a powder and as ready-mixed sports drinks. As a drink, they combine the advantages of liquids, being readily emptied from the stomach into the small intestine, but with the slower absorption that is usually found in solid carbohydrates.

There has been little work on the effects of fats and protein eaten during the exercise period. Fats improve the taste of snacks and thus may be helpful in counteracting the natural depression of appetite that occurs with exercise, but delays in stomach emptying can lead to nausea if the fats are taken in large amounts. The same is true for proteins, but to a lesser degree.

In 1984, White and his associates analyzed the diet of an ultra-distance bicyclist during a 24-hour event. They found that the percentage of total energy derived from proteins (10 percent) and fats (30 percent) decreased, with a marked shift toward carbohydrates (60 percent). This compares with the more "normal" pattern of 15 percent protein, 40 percent fat, and 45 percent carbohydrate found in the average diet. There was also an increase in the intake of liquids, with semisolid (36 percent) and liquid foods (30 percent) providing more than half the Calories. This shift was a result of the increased fluid requirements of exercise and a decrease in abdominal discomfort with the liquid diet.

As a rule of thumb, the higher the level of intensity of the ride (closer to your VO2max), the simpler the carbohydrate (energy drinks, gels, fruits). On longer rides at lower heart rates, more complex snacks with complex carbohydrates and a higher fat content offer other alternatives. A reasonable goal during high-intensity rides is 200 to 300 Calories (60 grams of carbohydrate) per hour.

Post-exercise Nutrition

Most amateur athletes fail to appreciate the importance of nutrition in the post-exercise period and feel that after a long training ride or competitive event, the only diet issue is planning the carbohydrate loading for the next session. The unappreciated secret is that successful carbohydrate loading begins as you are getting off the bike.

There is a four-hour "glycogen window" immediately after exercise during which any oral carbohydrates are converted into muscle glycogen at more than three times the normal rate. It also appears that "the earlier the better," as some data suggests a 50-percent fall in the glycogen conversion rate after 2 hours and a complete return to normal glycogen resynthesis rates after 4 hours. After this 4-hour window, muscle glycogen is replaced at a rate of 5 percent per hour. Although it may require up to 48 hours for complete muscle glycogen replacement, most restocking is accomplished during the initial 24 hours after the event.

The athlete who is training daily or is involved in a multi-day event can use this glycogen window to their advantage in getting a jump on the normal repletion process, minimizing the risk of chronic glycogen depletion and the fatigue that goes along with it. There is some evidence that the muscle stiffness that occurs after vigorous exercise may be related to muscle glycogen depletion. Rapid repletion may have the added benefit of minimizing this "day after" effect.

As in pre-event carbohydrate loading, an intake of 600 grams of carbohydrate in the 24 hours after the event achieves optimal results. Drinking a 100-gram liquid carbohydrate drink immediately after exercise, and repeating it 2 hours later, takes maximum advantage of this glycogen window. At that point, switching to solid complex carbohydrates (starches) may be superior to glucose in speedily completing the glycogen repletion process.

Although some muscle breakdown occurs with all vigorous exercise, the normal American diet contains more than enough protein to provide the raw materials for any repairs necessary in the post-exercise period.

Water/Fluids

Although water does not provide any Calories, adequate hydration is at least as important to good athletic performance as the food you eat. Perhaps the single biggest mistake of many competitive athletes is the failure to replace the fluid losses associated with exercise. This is especially so in bicycling because rapid skin evaporation decreases the sense of perspiring. This gives a false sense of minimal fluid loss, even though sweat production and imperceptible loss through the lungs can easily exceed 2 quarts per hour.

It is essential that fluid replacement begin early and continue on a regular basis. In fact, a South African study of two groups of bicyclists (one rehydrating, the other not) exercising at 90 percent VO2max demonstrated a measurable difference in physical performance as early as 15 minutes into the study. Serious fluid deficiencies occurred with minimal awareness on the part of the athletes, again pointing out that the sensation of thirst lags well behind the body's needs.

Total body fluid losses during exercise result in a decrease in plasma volume (the fluid circulating within the blood vessels), as well as muscle water content. As fluid loss progresses, there is a direct effect on physiological function and athletic performance. Unreplaced water loss of 2 percent of body weight begins to impact heat regulation; at 3 percent there is a measurable effect on muscle cell contraction times; and when fluid loss reaches 4 percent of body weight, there is a measurable 5- to 10-percent drop in performance. This effect on performance can persist up to 4 hours after rehydration takes place. Maintaining plasma volume is another one of the hidden keys to optimal physical performance. A successful fluid replacement program needs to begin at the same time as the ride, anticipating and regularly replacing fluid losses.

But don't assume that if a little is good, a lot is better. There are risks associated with overcorrecting the water losses of exercise. Hyponatremia (low blood sodium concentration) with seizures has been reported in marathon runners as a result of the overreplacement of the sweat losses (salt and water) with water alone. This is a particular risk for events of more than 5 hours. Weighing yourself regularly on long rides may help you tailor your replacement program. A weight gain of more that one or two pounds indicates that you are overcorrecting and might be placing yourself at risk for hyponatremia.

Under normal conditions, a minimum of four to five ounces of fluid should be taken every 15 minutes. When extreme conditions of heat and humidity are anticipated, remember the following strategies:

1. **Hydrate Before, During, and After the Ride.** Thirst is inadequate to stimulate complete rehydration, so learn to drink before you are thirsty. Using a CamelBak or similar device on long rides will let you drink without worrying about the need to stop, and risk losing your group.
2. **Don't Skimp When Using a Sports Drink.** Don't assume that because they contain electrolytes and carbohydrates, you don't need to drink as much. The sweet taste often keeps you from drinking, so take an extra bottle of plain water to alternate. Keeping fluids cool helps, so add ice or freeze half a bottle the night before, and top it off with water or extra sports drink just before the ride.
3. **Weigh Yourself Before and After the Ride.** Most of your weight loss will be fluid (two pounds equals 1 quart). A drop of a pound or two won't impair performance, but a greater drop indicates the need to reassess your personal program. And for rides of 5 hours or more, beware that a gain of more than 1 or 2 pounds could indicate you have overcompensated.
4. **Wear the Right Clothing.** Recommended are light colors to reflect heat, a loose weave jersey, and shorts made of one of the new "wicking" materials.
5. **Wear Your Helmet.** Modern, well-vented helmets funnel the wind onto your head, act to insulate your head from the sun's rays, and are actually cooler than your bare head.

The stomach does have its limits, however, and it appears that 800 milliliters, or approximately 1 quart, is near the upper limit of volume that is easily handled per hour. And this volume will decrease as exercise approaches 100 percent VO2max and gastric emptying slows. If larger volumes are pushed, nausea and stomach distention will result. A regular water bottle is 480 milliliters (16 ounces or 1/2 a quart), and the large ones are 750 milliliters. You should be able to drink at least two bottles per hour in hot conditions.

Sports Drinks

Sports drinks, which are really just high carbohydrate liquids, can be helpful in rides of more than two hours duration. The body's glycogen stores will support vigorous exercise for up to two hours before glycogen depletion and fatigue occur and any supplemental carbohydrates ingested during this period will spare muscle glycogen. Although this additional carbohydrate will not increase maximal performance levels, they will prolong the duration of exercise before exhaustion occurs. To put this into perspective, drinking a 10-percent glucose solution, equivalent to a regular cola or similar soft drink, at a rate of one quart per hour, would provide an additional 260 Calories. For a 165-

pound bicyclist riding at 15 miles per hour and expending 400 Calories per hour, this would provide a 50-percent increase in endurance. Sports drinks are also a convenient way to supplement the training diet and to restock glycogen stores in the four-hour post exercise replacement interval.

Liquids are readily emptied from the stomach. Any sugar they contain is quickly absorbed into the bloodstream and transported to the muscles. In the muscles, it is readily available as an alternative to muscle glycogen as an energy source. Following the same reasoning, drinks containing glucose polymers (increasing Calories while remaining isoosmotic) are of additional benefit, delivering additional Calories per ounce of fluid.

No studies have confirmed a benefit of fruit drinks containing the sugar fructose when compared with the sugar glucose. Although fructose requires less insulin to enter muscle cells, this does not appear to provide a performance advantage in bicycling. Taste alone is the only advantage.

For many years it was believed that a 2.5-percent concentration of glucose or glucose polymer molecules was the maximum tolerated without risking a delay in stomach emptying and nausea. But numerous studies in bicyclists have demonstrated normal gastric emptying with 6 to 8 percent solutions, with nausea occurring only when using concentrations above 11 percent. Interestingly, the old standbys such as apple juice and cola drinks have a sugar concentration of 10 percent. Even though the glucose polymer sports drinks can provide more Calories per quart at the same overall concentration, careful studies have not demonstrated any performance advantage over the simple sugar solutions alone. The major benefit of the polymers appear to be the absence of the sweet taste and nauseating properties of the high-concentration glucose drinks, which can be a barrier to maintaining a high fluid intake.

Although most research has analyzed solutions with a sugar concentration of 6 to 8 percent, there is some research that concentrations of up to 20 to 25 percent may be well-tolerated by athletes who have used them regularly in training. This is particularly important for ultra-endurance athletes who expend thousands of Calories per day and, as a result, have great difficulty meeting their energy replacement requirements.

In one 2-hour study at 70 percent VO2max, with average fluid losses of 2,300 milliliters, there was no discernible advantage of electrolyte drinks over water alone. However, when larger fluid volumes need to be replaced, taste and digestive tract tolerance are increasingly important considerations in the selection of replacement fluids. And the larger the volumes, the more important electrolyte replacement becomes in preventing dilutional hyponatremia.

In summary, drinking plain water at a rate of 1 quart per hour is adequate for rides of 1 1/2 to 2 hours. On longer rides, where the body's glycogen stores will be approaching exhaustion, liquid carbohydrate supplements assume increased importance. Glucose-containing liquids can deliver Calories from the mouth to the muscles in as little as 10 minutes, compared to solid foods and energy bars which empty more slowly from the stomach. In most individuals, an 8- to 10-percent concentration appears to be the maximum tolerated.

Glucose polymers offer the advantage of increasing the total concentration of Calories per quart, without the side effect of an unpalatable, sweet taste. But otherwise, glucose polymers have no advantage over simple sugar (glucose) drinks during a ride. Although there are many commercial drinks available, the old standbys such as apple juice and cola drinks are probably the least expensive per Calorie provided. However, in the before and after ride period, the high Calorie, easily-absorbed glucose polymer sports drinks are ideal for building or restocking glycogen stores.

There have been some encouraging studies on the use of glycerol (see chapter 5) to minimize the negative impact of dehydration on performance. But at this time there are still unresolved questions as to harmful effects, and there are no commercial products available.

Recovery Drinks

Immediately after a ride, the enzymes responsible for replenishing carbohydrates in the muscles and liver are most active. The athlete that trains daily, or rides in a multi-day event, can use this glycogen window to his or her advantage to get a jump on the normal repletion process. They can also minimize the chance of chronic glycogen depletion and the fatigue that goes along with it. Recovery drinks are advertised as taking particular advantage of this glycogen window.

The standard recommendation is to drink or eat 200 grams of carbohydrate during this 4-hour period. One study suggested that cyclists who drank a beverage containing both carbohydrates and protein replenished muscle glycogen levels 38 percent faster than with a carbohydrate drink alone.

There are numerous recovery drinks available, but they are expensive. It has been estimated that if you had one serving a day, six days a week, the annual cost would be $1,000 per year or more. So if you are designing your own drink, or choosing from one of the commercial products, remember these guidelines:

1. Make sure you like the taste.
2. Aim for three to four grams of carbohydrate for every gram of protein.
3. Choose a liquid that contains quickly absorbed sugars such as glucose, sucrose, or maltodextrin as the first few ingredients.
4. Remember that the benefit of recovery ingredients such as ginseng, carnitine,

chromium, and inosine, to name a few, are unproved. And the same is true of vitamins if you are eating a well-balanced diet.

And, in reality, having a soft drink to cool down may be just as helpful and a lot less expensive.

Sports Bars

Commercial sports bars are almost entirely carbohydrates (of varying types), although a few have been pushing their fat content as well. They almost always contain "special" supplements (see chapter 5). Their advantage over cookies or other snacks is that they are prepackaged, are readily available in bike shops, and offer another taste and texture option. But as a source of energy, they are no more effective on a gram-for-gram basis as an energy booster than other carbohydrate snacks.

Energy Gels

Energy gels are the latest alternative to the often hard-to-unwrap, difficult-to-chew, and relatively tasteless commercial energy bars. These gels are syrups or pastes containing a combination of simple and complex carbohydrates, usually maltodextrin, rice syrup, or oligosaccharides. They are packaged in a palm-sized packet of plastic or foil with a tear-off end, allowing the contents to be "sucked" out rather than chewed. They contain from 70 to 100 Calories per packet (from 17 to 25 grams of carbohydrate) and are usually fat-free. If you were aiming for 60 grams of carbohydrate per hour to supplement muscle glycogen supplies, you would need a gel packet every 30 minutes.

Being semiliquid, they do offer the advantage of emptying more quickly from the stomach and potentially providing a more rapid energy boost than solid sports bars. But studies comparing solid and gel carbohydrate supplements have yet to be published. And in a study of the more traditional solid versus liquid carbohydrate supplements, bicycling performance was similar in two groups of bicyclists. One group was using equal amounts of water and carbohydrate consumed as a sports drink, and the other a solid sports bar and water. This suggests that, aside from taste and ease of use, energy gels are a relatively pricey snack with little to recommend them over bagels or fig newtons as a carbohydrate supplement.

You can even make your own gel. Two or three tablespoons of runny jam or fruit syrup will provide about 25 grams of carbohydrate. Just look for a product that lists glucose or sucrose as the first ingredient and buy a refillable plastic tube from a camping or athletic store. Likewise, a tablespoon of Karo syrup contains 15 grams (60 Calories) of pure carbohydrate and can be flavored with Tang or Kool-Aid crystals at a fraction of the cost of commercial energy gels.

Are they worth it? It really depends on personal preference. Some riders cannot chew and swallow a sports bar while pedaling. Others develop taste fatigue to sports drinks on long rides. For these individuals, gels provide an alternative. But aside from taste, there are no proven performance advantages, and they are expensive if used regularly on long rides.

The Bottom Line

There are three practical points for bicyclists to remember when developing their own dietary training program.

First, the body's normal liver and muscle glycogen stores will support the first 1 to 2 hours of exercise at 70 percent VO2 max without any need for supplementation. And both a good training program to improve the muscle efficiency of the individual as well as riding or exercising at a reasonable pace will postpone the onset of glycogen depletion and fatigue.

Second, taking in carbohydrates during the event provides an additional source of glucose Calories that will extend the length of time before the bonk occurs. This assumes importance for rides of greater than 2 hours. As a general rule, the body can utilize 60 grams of absorbed carbohydrate per hour to supplement muscle glycogen stores and the stomach can handle between 1 and 2 quarts of fluid before nausea occurs. This does put an upper limit on liquid carbohydrate supplementation during a ride. But there is no problem in also using some solid foods, as long as enough fluids are taken with them.

Finally, eating a high-carbohydrate diet for several days prior to the event, and utilizing the 4-hour post-ride glycogen window, will maximize internal carbohydrate stores, prolonging the duration of the activity until fatigue occurs.

CHAPTER FIVE

Nutritional Supplements and Alternatives

Fiber

Dietary fiber has received considerable attention during the last few years. In the diet, fiber refers to nondigestible carbohydrates such as cellulose, lignin, and pectin found in fruits, grains, and vegetables. Fiber provides bulk to assist in regular elimination. There is evidence that population groups with a traditionally low-fiber diet also have an increased incidence of diverticulosis, cardiovascular disease, colon cancer, and diabetes.

There are no special dietary fiber requirements for bicyclists or other athletes. But there is evidence that too much fiber may bind minerals such as iron, resulting in poor absorption. Personal anecdotes on GI distress, specifically bloating, from a high-fiber diet are common.

The most reasonable approach is a well-balanced diet with enough fruits, grains, and vegetables to maintain regular bowel function.

Pritikin Diet

The concept of a high-carbohydrate diet is pushed to its limits by the Pritikin diet. This diet, or rather eating program, stresses a high intake of complex carbohydrates (75 percent to 80 percent of total Calories) and a marked reduction in fat and protein (each contributing about 10 percent).

In his writings, Robert Pritikin relates numerous testimonials from triathletes and other endurance athletes to support his claims of improved athletic performance. His concept, which amounts to continuous carbohydrate loading, is supported by the principles of athletic nutrition as outlined in the previous chapter. It's at the opposite end of the dietary spectrum from Barry Sear's high-fat diet, as proposed in his book, *The Zone*. Aside from the somewhat monotonous nature of the meal plans, Pritikin's regimen is a reasonable option for the athlete in training as well as for those who feel a need to modify the high-fat western diet. Whether or not it actually improves athletic performance is as yet unresolved.

Vegetarian Diets

A growing number of bicyclists are adopting vegetarian and red meat-free life style. Not only are vegetarians healthier, with lower rates of heart disease, obesity, and colon cancer, but the fact that their diets are high in carbohydrates means they are constantly "carbo loaded." In many ways, this is just a Pritikin diet without any lean meat.

There are a few tips to remember if you are considering this dietary lifestyle change. Vegans, who eat no animal products whatsoever, not even dairy products, need to be certain they get enough of the following: vitamin B12 from supplements and fortified foods such as cereal, bread, pasta, and brewer's yeast; iron from beans, kale, dried fruit, and collard greens; and calcium from dark leafy vegetables, broccoli, and citrus fruits.

It is important to make sure there is an appropriate balance of proteins. Because certain essential amino acids are not found in all proteins, a conscious effort needs to be made to eat complementary protein foods in the same meal or in consecutive meals. Doing so will provide the proper balance of amino acid building blocks for building and repairing tissue. Examples of complementary proteins are pinto beans with rice, and grains such as rice, bread, and cereal with legumes such as peas or beans.

And vegans need to eat a bit more than if they were using meat as a protein source. For example, a 3-ounce piece of meat which contains 21 grams of protein is equivalent to a cup of cooked grain and a cup of cooked beans.

Vitamins

Vitamins act as catalysts in the metabolic steps that convert fat, carbohydrate, and protein Calories into ATP to fuel muscle activity. As catalysts, they facilitate the metabolic conversion but are not "used up" or consumed in the process. For that reason, the recommended daily requirements (RDA) are similar in all individuals and are independent of daily energy requirements.

Vitamins are usually considered a safe and effective way to improve performance. They are often recommended by coaches and trainers, but multiple studies of body tissue vitamin levels in athletes have failed to identify any specific deficiencies in those on a balanced diet replacing training Calories. It has been alleged that athletes need higher than normal dietary levels of vitamins to maintain maximum performance, but there is no evidence to support improved performance, even with high dose supplementation that raises the corresponding blood levels.

There is evidence that megavitamin programs can be harmful. The fat soluble vitamins A, D, E, and K are not easily eliminated from the body and can accumulate in body fatty tissues to reach toxic levels. And there have been reports that even the water-soluble vitamins, B complex and C, which are excreted in the urine when excess amounts are taken, can be harmful when taken at doses of 10 to 100 times the RDA.

If you are concerned about your diet being well-balanced, there is no harm in using a simple over-the-counter multiple vitamin once a day. But vitamins are not an easy answer to increased performance.

Minerals

Minerals are found in the body either in their elemental form or combined with organic compounds. Like vitamins, they are essential for normal cell functioning. The two most prevalent minerals, calcium and phosphorus, are major components of bone. Sodium and potassium are found in the water that is both within and around cells. Magnesium, chloride, sulfur, and zinc play a key role in cell function. The trace elements iron, manganese, copper, and iodine are found in much smaller quantities, but play essential roles as catalysts in basic cellular chemical processes.

One of the most plentiful minerals in the body is sodium chloride, or table salt. Over a 24-hour period, the athlete's standard training diet replaces two to three times the normal salt losses. Only under extreme environmental conditions of high temperature or high humidity is a salt supplement needed. An exception may be the bicyclist who has not trained for an event and can lose excessive amounts of salt in perspiration. Although exercise cramps were once thought to be a result of salt deficiency, it now appears that they are actually a heat cramp related to dehydration and a decreased blood flow to the muscles.

Calcium is the major mineral involved in bone growth and repair. There is no evidence to support use of calcium supplements in the active athlete, with the exception of female athletes who, because of the intensity of their training, become amenorrheic. Amenorrhea is the abnormal suppression of the menstrual cycle, and is associated with hormonal changes that can affect bone formation. Recent evidence has suggested that the positive effects of exercise on bone formation in all athletes will act to minimize the hormonal effects of amenorrhea in this group as well, and at this time there is no consensus on the need for calcium supplements.

Iron needs have been studied extensively in athletes. A deficiency state does occur on occasion and results in a negative effect on performance. Once again, this is more of a problem for the woman athlete, because of the additional iron needed to replace menstrual blood loss. When the U.S. Olympic team was studied, it was found that 20 to 30 percent of the female athletes did not get adequate iron in their diet alone. But iron is toxic in excessive amounts, so any question as to a deficiency state should be resolved with a screening blood count, and serum iron or ferritin assay, before starting routine supplements.

Found in all foods, minerals are kept in balance by regulation of both their absorption and excretion. Adequate tissue levels of minerals are easily maintained by a balanced diet. As with vitamins, studies of tissue levels in athletes have failed to identify mineral deficiencies on a balanced diet. And with the exception of iron in athletes who were clearly anemic, studies of mineral supplementation have failed to demonstrate an improvement in performance. Since most minerals have toxic side effects, only calcium (for long-term bone strength) and iron (in clearly deficient individuals) are recommended as occasional supplements.

Antioxidants

Free radicals are chemically reactive molecules produced by external factors such as cigarette smoke and environmental pollution, which are blamed for everything from premature aging and heart disease to cancer. Recently it has been suggested that free radicals may even contribute to a slow recovery after tough rides. Antioxidants are chemical compounds, generally the vitamins C, E, and beta carotene, that neutralize free radicals.

Exercise does increase the rate of lipid peroxidation (the formation of free radicals), but there is also a rise in the natural antioxidant activity in the blood. And with regular training, this antioxidant defense system is even more effective. Unfortunately, there is little data as to where the balance lies: in favor of the free radicals or the body's defenses. These studies suggest that the "weekend warriors" who don't have a regular training program are the more susceptible to free radical damage.

Short-term studies in athletes are more controversial, but at least one has suggested that the use of antioxidants in the form of vitamins C, E, and beta carotene decreased microscopic muscle damage in a group of runners compared with a control group. There are numerous anecdotal reports that vitamin C taken before a ride diminished the amount of muscle soreness the next day. The only controlled studies were with 600 IU (international units) of vitamin E for two days before exercise (no effect) and a second with three grams of vitamin C per day for three days before and four days after an exercise bout (reduced soreness). However, at recommended doses, none of the antioxidant vitamins have shown a beneficial effect on exercise performance or the rate of post-exercise recovery in well-fed athletes. Megadoses, because of side effects, will definitely decrease physical performance.

There is some evidence supporting the longer-term benefits of antioxidants. A study of nurses and male professionals published in 1993 did demonstrate a lower rate of heart disease in those taking Vitamin E supplements. A study from China indicated that the use of a multivitamin, containing antioxidants among other things, lowered the cancer death rate by 13 percent. However, a recent 1996 study indicated the opposite: Patients at risk for lung cancer had a higher cancer rate if they took beta carotene supplements. The study was terminated early because of those results.

The bottom line is that there is very little evidence to support the short-term benefit of antioxidants for the competitive athlete and plenty of controversy as to any long-term health benefits. There is general agreement that natural sources of these micronutrients are more effective than the vitamins you buy in a bottle. Increasing the fruits and vegetables in your diet might be a good compromise if you feel you'd like to give them a try. And if you do opt for the recommended doses of vitamin supplements, only your pocketbook would appear to be at risk.

Here are some specifics on antioxidants:

Vitamin C
- Food sources: citrus fruits, potato, broccoli, cauliflower, cabbage, watermelon, cantaloupe
- RDA: 60 milligrams per day (1 orange, 1/2 cup broccoli)
- Supplement: 250–500 milligrams per day
- Warnings: More than 500 milligrams can cause diarrhea

Vitamin E
- Food sources: vegetable oil, nuts, wheat germ, margarine, seeds, leafy greens, asparagus
- RDA: 8-10 milligrams per day (4–5 ounces of peanuts)
- Supplement: 200-800 IU
- Warnings: No serious side effects in the doses recommended

Vitamin A
- Food sources: milk, cheese, egg, liver, fish oil
- RDA: 800–1,000 micrograms
- Supplement: None; your body will convert beta carotene safely into vitamin A
- Warnings: Toxic (even lethal) at high doses

Beta Carotene
- Food sources: carrots, cantaloupe, squash, sweet potato, spinach
- RDA: None, but 5–6 milligrams are suggested (1/2 carrot)
- Supplement: 6–15 milligrams per day
- Warnings: Not toxic, but in high doses your skin may turn yellow (carotenemia)

Ergogenic aids
Competitive cyclists who have achieved maximal results from their training programs will often turn to extrinsic aids (termed ergogenic aids) to enhance their performance. These include psychological aids, such as hypnosis and psychothera-

53

py; pharmacological aids, such as erythropoietin; and nutritional supplements, such as creatine phosphate, vitamins, and minerals.

The use of performance-enhancing dietary supplements can be traced at least as far back as the Romans, who reportedly drank lion's blood to improve their strength and courage. Unfortunately nutritional supplements are frequently promoted with unsubstantiated claims in magazine advertisements and health food stores, by coaches, and by entrepreneurs who stand to gain financially from their use.

There are three common flaws in these claims: (1) an absence of a "control" group using an inert or inactive agent in multisubject studies, (2) the use of anecdotal or personal testimonials, and (3) a failure to understand the strengths and weaknesses of statistics in sorting out conflicting results. As a result, a placebo effect is often confused with a real and reproducible benefit of a supplement.

A placebo is an inert compound, identical in appearance with the active compound being tested, that is used in experimental research with both the subject groups and the experimenter unaware of which group is administered the active compound. The placebo effect results from our optimism and hope that a medication, supplement, or training program will be beneficial; this biases us toward a positive impression of the results even if the supplement is ineffective or inactive. This is best demonstrated when a sugar pill (the placebo) is used in studying disease treatments. When told that the placebo will help, a large percentage of subjects report significant benefits. However, this beneficial effect lasts for only a few doses.

We can eliminate a placebo effect by comparing two groups of athletes in carefully monitored or "controlled" studies, with one group using the active ingredient and the other given an inactive or sham ingredient (the placebo). In the best studies, even the investigators are kept in the dark as to which group had the active agent (a doubly blinded or double-blind study). Only by meticulous studies such as these can we eliminate our own biases in the use of these diet supplements.

The placebo effect explains why an athlete, using a product without a blinded, inactive comparison, and giving a testimonial based on his or her own perception of its benefit, will almost always report the results in a positive way.

Good clinical studies use statistical methods to sort out the reproducible effects (positive or negative) of a supplement. But even in the best of studies, the potential remains for random, nonreproducible results. So if you find several studies, with only one supporting a positive or beneficial effect, be skeptical as the single positive result may have been by chance alone, and thus not reproducible. Likewise, be wary of the single, often-quoted study with results that no one else can duplicate.

It is important to put these numerous claims into perspective. An improvement of a few percent, obtained in repetitive sprints to exhaustion on a bike trainer in a laboratory, may have little relevance to you as an endurance or recreational athlete.

The underlying theme of this section is to remain open-minded yet skeptical about seemingly unbelievable claims for these products. Unless they are proven with well-designed, blinded studies, assume that a claim which sounds too good to be true probably is. There are few shortcuts for a well-designed conditioning program supported with sound nutrition. Although there may be little risk in trying supplements, there is a dollar cost for those on a limited budget and the potential to lose focus on the role of a good training program.

As might be imagined, the list of nutritional supplements advocated as ergogenic aids is extensive. I've tried to identify those that are clearly helpful and beneficial for improving bicycling performance, and to address a few of the popular myths as well. Whenever possible, the original scientific studies were reviewed to validate the claims.

Alcohol

Occasional articles tout the benefits of alcohol as an energy source for sports activities. Although alcohol does contain more energy per gram (7 Cal/gram) than carbohydrates, and is rapidly absorbed from the intestinal tract, evidence suggests these Calories are not utilized to any significant extent during exercise. And its negative effects, including the facts that it is a diuretic and contributes to dehydration; it slows down glucose production and release from the liver; and it disturbs motor skills including balance and coordination, outweigh any theoretical positive ones.

In a recent study at Penn State, 10 women were given a mixed cocktail equal to a moderate alcoholic drink. They then rode stationary bikes for 30 minutes at 70 percent of their maximum heart rate. Compared to their own baseline performance off alcohol, bicycling after alcohol required more energy, produced a higher heart rate, and stimulated a higher cardiovascular demand. Even moderate drinking while exercising placed increased demands on the cardiovascular system. The bottom line was a definite negative influence on performance.

Amino Acids

Purified amino acids (particularly arginine, ornithine, lysine, and tyrosine) have become popular, if expensive, forms of protein supplementation. Five well-performed studies have failed to demonstrate that either singly, or in combination, is there any significant effect on muscular development, strength, or power.

Amino acids are the building blocks of proteins and are present in all foods. As with vitamins, a balanced diet should provide more than enough of the essential amino acids. The amino acids sold in the health food store for $20 to $30 per bottle have no proven advantage over a glass of milk and a peanut butter sandwich, and they don't have nearly the taste appeal. In addition, too much protein in the diet has a diuretic effect that increases the risk of dehydration. Excessive protein can also cause diarrhea, abdominal bloating and, by placing an additional burden on the kidneys, may lead to chronic renal damage. Because an increase in carbohydrates, particularly during training, has a protein-sparing effect, there is another alternative: adding jelly to the peanut butter sandwich!

Caffeine

Caffeine is a member of a group of compounds called methylxanthines found naturally in coffee beans, tea leaves, chocolate, cocoa beans, guarana, and cola (kola) nuts.

During prolonged exercise, the onset of fatigue correlates closely with the depletion of muscle glycogen stores (and is delayed if glycogen is spared). The metabolism of free fatty acids (FFAs) as an alternative energy source can decrease the use of muscle glycogen. Caffeine will increase blood FFAs, and it is felt that this is its major method of action. In one study, caffeine produced a 50-percent increase in FFA at 3 to 4 hours. This effect was seen after 300 milligrams of caffeine. An average 6-ounce cup of brewed coffee contains 100 to 150 milligrams of caffeine.

There is speculation that some of caffeine's benefits may be related to its central nervous system effect as a stimulant and a recent study has demonstrated a direct, positive effect on the muscle fiber itself with a reported 7-percent increase in power output over a 6-second cycle exercise task.

In one controlled study, subjects were able to perform for 90 minutes to fatigue as compared to 75 minutes in controls (a 20-percent increase) after drinking the equivalent of three cups of coffee or six caffeinated colas 1 hour before, even though values for heart rate and oxygen uptake were similar in both groups. Another study, looking at performance with acute altitude change (4,300 meters or 14,000 feet), demonstrated a 50-percent increase in performance with caffeine supplements. How this would help at lesser elevations, riding in the Rocky Mountains, for example, is not clear.

A suggested dose of caffeine for the recreational rider is 5 milligrams per kilogram of body weight. This dose can be taken 1 hour before the ride or, if you prefer, in smaller doses periodically throughout the ride itself.

But there are occasional side effects. Caffeine can cause headaches, insomnia, and nervous irritability. In addition, it is a potent diuretic and can lead to dehydration. However, the biggest negative is that in high concentrations, it is considered a drug and is banned by the U.S. Olympic Committee and U.S. Cycling Federation. To exceed the U.S. Cycling Federation's legal limit for caffeine, which is a urine concentration of 12 micrograms per milliliter, one would have to ingest 600 milligrams of caffeine and have a urine test within 2 to 3 hours.

Most endurance athletes consider caffeine beneficial if used correctly. This includes a period of abstinence for several weeks before the event, as habitual use induces a tolerance to its positive effects.

Citrate

Sodium citrate, a chemical compound, was evaluated in a 30-kilometer, high-intensity time trial event at a dose of 0.5 grams per kilogram of body weight. Total power output, but not peak power output, was greater in this treated group. At 30 kilometers, the riders using sodium citrate had an average 100-second lead. The bicyclists using the sodium citrate had a higher venous blood pH throughout the ride, and it is presumed that this buffering effect led to the improved performance (by optimizing the pH within the muscle cell and enhancing contractility).

Sodium citrate has also been shown to increase peak power over a placebo control group during short, high-intensity cycle ergometry of 120 and 240 seconds duration. Again, this is thought to be related to optimizing the pH within the active muscle cell.

Creatine

Creatine is an organic compound which, combined with phosphate, yields creatine phosphate, an intermediary in the energy transfer cycle in the cell. Creatine is available commercially in the form of creatine monohydrate. As a supplement, it increases body weight. Whether this is related to water retention or the development of true muscle mass is still unproved. It improves performance during maximal strength or power tests (weight lifting) or in repetitive, high-intensity exercise with short recovery intervals (short sprints of 5- to 15-second duration). No short-term toxicity has been reported at doses of 20 to 30 grams per day; however, there are some questions as to whether long-term use of high doses might affect the kidneys.

This compound is probably effective in limited situations. It is doubtful that it is of any benefit for a single sprint of any duration. The one study closest to a real-life bicycling situation, an 18-mile time trial that included six 15-second sprints, demonstrated no difference between riders receiving creatine or a placebo. So if you are being beaten by competitors using this supplement, it is probably for other reasons.

Glycerol

A chemical compound that along with fatty acids forms triglycerides, glycerol is a clear, syrupy, and extremely sweet substance, which also has water-retaining effects when taken orally. In 1987, it was shown that resting subjects who drank a glycerol solution retained 50 percent more fluid than drinking a similar volume of water alone. This led to investigation of its ability to help prevent dehydration under extreme conditions of exercise, heat, and high humidity.

A follow-up study in 1990 demonstrated that subjects preloaded with a glycerol solution did sweat at a greater rate with exercise. But remember, they started out with an excess of total body water from the water retention effects. Overall, the glycerol group demonstrated a net positive effect on fluid balance (less plasma volume depletion) while maintaining a lower core body temperature, which was presumably a combination of more efficient circulation from the increased plasma volume and the higher rate of heat dissipation with perspiration.

In 1992, 11 bicyclists rode to exhaustion at 60 percent VO2 max. The group that prehydrated with a glycerol/water mix improved their endurance by 22 percent (94 versus 77 minutes) over the water-alone group. A repeat study used the same prehydration approach, but added a replacement program (while riding) of water alone for the pure water prehydration group versus a sports drink for the glycerol prehydrated group. The results revealed an even greater advantage of 32 percent (93 minutes for water alone versus 123 minutes with the glycerol and sports drink regimen). And this has been supported with a third study which prehydrated one group with glycerol (1.2 grams glycerol per kilogram of body weight in a total volume of 5 milliliters per kilogram of body weight) 1 hour before a ride at 60-percent VO2max. Both groups (glycerol pretreated, pure water) drank 9 milliliters per kilogram per hour of a 5 percent dextrose solution during the ride. The glycerol pretreated group increased their time to exhaustion by 24 percent.

Possible side effects include headache and nausea, which could hinder overall performance for any individual. However, the side effects appear to be unusual if proper concentrations are used. One researcher, who has used glycerol on 200 subjects, reports that only 2 or 3 did not tolerate it. It should be considered a potential performance enhancer for any ride lasting an hour or more, particularly under the adverse conditions of high heat and humidity.

However, several recent papers presented at the American College of Sports Medicine (1997) failed to show any difference between pre-ride hyperhydration with glycerol versus water alone in terms of time to exhaustion. And to top it off, glycerol has recently been banned by international cycling's governing body, the UCI.

Herbs

The biggest shortcoming of herbs and herb teas is the inability to identify the active ingredients, increasing the possibility of taking a substance banned by the International Olympic Committee or the U.S. Olympic Committee. Strength of teas is directly related to the brewing time, making calculation of a "safe" dose difficult and increasing the chances of a toxic side effect.

Astragalus is a root herb from the Mongolian wilderness reported to increase the body's capacity to handle stress, help reduce fatigue, and enhance endurance. There are no studies with specifics on the herb, and all information is purely anecdotal.

Ciwujia is an herb derived from a root grown in the northeast section of China. It has been used in traditional Chinese medicine for over 1,700 years to treat fatigue and bolster the immune system. Commercially prepared and marketed under the trade name Endurox in the United States, it is claimed to shift energy metabolism in the exercising muscle from carbohydrate to fat, thus sparing carbohydrate and slowing lactic acid build-up, and to decrease heart rate during moderate exercise.

However, the basic research is in the Chinese literature and was done only on animals. The human research done in the United States has not been published—and probably won't be—as it wasn't done in a blinded, controlled fashion. The exercise was of only moderate intensity, and the longest exercise bout lasted 60 minutes. So for the moment, there is no proof that this supplement is of any benefit to athletes exercising near their VO2max or for prolonged times at moderate intensity.

Ginsengs are herbal preparations extracted from the roots of plants in the family Araliaceae, and contain a wide variety of chemical substances. Thus, all ginsengs are not equivalent, as far as ergogenic potential. Some may work at the higher centers of the central nervous system to enhance both mental and physical stamina.

A commonly advertised commercial product, Ginsana, claims to produce lower lactate levels and increase VO2max. However, as with many of the herbal products, there are as many studies supporting the claims as refuting them . . . a common situation with ineffective claims. And the most recent, which are the most carefully controlled, failed to demonstrate any change in maximal aerobic performance after two and three weeks of supplementation. At recommended doses, ginseng can produce the "ginseng abuse syndrome": high blood pressure, nervousness, and confusion. Although this compound may be considered as possibly effective, it does need further study.

Guarana is a South American herb used as a natural source of caffeine. The caffeine effect of one teaspoon (100 milligrams) of guarana is equivalent to one cup of coffee.

Ma Huang, a traditional Chinese herb tea, contains ephedra, a short-acting stimulant which mimics adrenaline. The synthetic version, ephedrine, is found in asthma and nasal decongestant (pseudoephedrine) products. It has been used in tandem with other natural caffeine sources such as kola nut and guarana. In higher doses it can cause tremors, rapid breathing, nervousness, and insomnia, common side effects of caffeine as well.

NUTRITIONAL SUPPLEMENTS AND ALTERNATIVES

Although it appears to be safe in small amounts (up to 50 milligrams of ephedrine or two cups of Ma Huang tea per day), with daily use a tolerance will develop and it will become less effective as time passes. Its use in any amount is banned by the International Olympic Committee. In fact the U.S. Olympic Committee advises athletes to eliminate all herb-based teas and diet supplements for one week prior to a race (and urine testing) if they are unsure whether they might contain ephedra. Likewise, check on any decongestant and asthma medications to see if they contain ephedrine.

Smilax Officinalis, native to the tropics of Brazil, began as a pharmaceutical base for the production of certain anabolic steroids. However, without the chemical modifications, Smilax Officinalis is thought to be nontoxic, and its use has no known negative side effects. It is alleged to raise the blood content of testosterone and to be equal to anabolic steroids in gains of lean muscle mass. However, these performance claims are not supported by published research studies.

Yohimbine is an alkaloid extracted from the bark of the yohimbe tree and claimed to have an anabolic effect through stimulating the release of testosterone or human growth hormone. Performance claims are not supported by published research studies.

Phosphate

A blood phosphate compound (2,3 diphosphoglycerate, or DPG) binds with hemoglobin to facilitate the release of oxygen at the level of the muscle capillary. Thus, oral phosphate, a building block of DPG, has been investigated as a performance enhancer. However, results have been conflicting, and although there is some suggestive evidence, this compound should be considered an unproven ergogenic aid at this time.

Usual doses are three to four grams of calcium or sodium phosphate for three to six days. Phosphate supplements may cause gastrointestinal distress unless consumed with ample fluids or food, and chronic consumption may interfere with calcium balance.

Sodium Bicarbonate

Available as baking soda or Alka Seltzer, sodium bicarbonate buffers lactic acid, allowing longer bouts of near maximal bicycling for short, high-intensity sprint events lasting from 1 to 7 minutes (400-meter or 800-meter sprints, time trials). But it adds little to the body's natural buffering capacity for lactic acid during very short, intense exercise lasting less than 30 seconds or sustained endurance events. Studies that used doses of 300 milligrams per kilogram of body weight found an ergogenic effect, while those using less than 200 milligrams per kilogram showed no effect.

One early study at Iowa State University demonstrated an improvement in sprinting ability after taking two tablespoons of baking soda immediately prior to the event. However, diarrhea and stomach upset were reported, and it appeared to be beneficial only in very short events such as the 4,000-meter pursuit. Another study demonstrated an increase in average power output on a cycle ergometer during repeated 10-second sprints. A third study at the University of Washington has failed to demonstrate any improvement in a series of 1-minute intervals at 95 percent VO2max in female bicyclists.

CHAPTER SIX

Nutrition for the Recreational Cyclist

I n this chapter we will apply the basic physiologic and nutritional concepts presented earlier to tailor a nutritional program for 1- to 2-hour rides of moderate intensity. These include social rides with your local bicycling group or friends, training rides of 15 to 50 miles, and bicycle commuting. As we plan a diet program, we will focus on the final four days of the training diet, the 4-hour pre-ride meal, supplements during the ride itself, and the 4-hour post-ride recovery period.

The Social and Commuter Ride

The recreational rider and commuter bicyclist will usually ride for an hour or two at 50 percent to 60 percent of their maximum (VO2max) with the goal of a comfortable ride with energy left over for the rest of the day.

Training diet requirements are minimal and are met with any balanced diet. Daily Calories should replace those expended, and 60 percent to 70 percent of the Calories should come from carbohydrates.

For rides of less than 2 hours, the pre-ride nutritional requirements are also flexible. If the training diet meets caloric needs, there will be more than adequate muscle glycogen even if the pre-ride meal is skipped. However, a breakfast high in carbohydrates will spare these muscle glycogen stores and lessen the chance of running out of gas later in the day. As the physical intensity of the ride is low, this meal can be eaten shortly before the ride with minimal risks of GI upset.

Carbohydrate supplements during the ride are also optional. As with the pre-ride meal, Calories eaten while on the bike will decrease the chance of fatigue from low glycogen stores later in the day. One water bottle of fluid per hour will eliminate any worries about dehydration.

Post-ride nutrition is particularly important if the pre-ride meal and snacks while biking were skipped. These carbohydrates will replace depleted glycogen reserves, minimizing the risk of weariness later in the day. This is a particular problem for daily riders, as failure to regularly replenish muscle glycogen stores on a daily basis increases the chance of chronic depletion andpost-ride fatigue.

The Basic Training Ride

This ride is also at a moderate pace but a bit too long to be completely covered by muscle glycogen stores. The pre-event meal and snacking on the bike are important to avoid the bonk. This ride is usually part of an ongoing training program, and the training diet needs to be monitored to avoid chronic glycogen depletion. If the ride will be above 60 percent VO2max, the 4-hour pre-ride fasting interval should be observed to minimize the chance of GI distress on the bike.

The training diet should meet daily caloric needs with 60 percent of Calories as carbohydrate, 15 percent protein, and 25 percent fat. Eating at least 600 grams of carbohydrate a day are recommended. As training intensifies and total caloric needs increase, the dietary carbohydrate Calories should increase as well, with fat and protein requirements left unchanged. As this shift occurs, it is not unusual for a regularly training rider to replace 75 to 80 percent of daily Calories in the form of carbohydrates. The daily program should be structured so that a significant percentage of the Calories are taken early in the day to anticipate the metabolic needs of the day's exercise.

To minimize the risks of the bonk, it is recommended that a low-fat pre-ride meal with 300 grams of carbohydrate be eaten 3 or 4 hours before the ride. A liquid meal will empty more quickly from the stomach and is preferred by some cyclists who feel it decreases nausea while riding.

The 45-gram carbohydrate snack immediately prior to the ride continues the carbohydrate supplementation that will protect muscle glycogen stores during exercise. It is important to time this snack, as eating a high-sugar snack too early increases the possibility that digestion, absorption, and an insulin response will lead to hypoglycemia just as the ride is beginning.

Once fatigue has occurred, oral glucose is much less effective in prolonging high-level aerobic activities, so on the bike, carbohydrate snacks—including energy gels and sports drinks—should be started with the ride. One gram of glucose per minute (four Calories per minute, 240 Calories per hour) is easily absorbed and metabolized during exercise, and some recent research suggests that complex carbohydrate drinks may increase this up to 800 Calories per hour.

Fluid replacement with a goal of at least one water bottle per hour should begin within 15 to 20 minutes of the start of the event, particularly if there are high temperatures or very high or low humidity.

Post-event nutrition is particularly important if a regular training ride is planned for the next day. A carbohydrate drink, especially a complex carbohydrate, in the 4 hours post-event takes advantage of the period of maximum glycogen resynthesis and may cut down on post-exercise muscle soreness.

Recommended Nutrition Plan: Moderate Activity—Up to 4 Hours

Four days prior to the ride
- balanced diet meeting daily Calorie needs with 60-70 percent of Calories as carbohydrates
- no specific recommendations for the occasional 1-2 hour ride
- 600 grams of carbohydrates the day before an extended 3-4 hour training ride

Four hours prior to the ride
- 300 gram carbohydrate meal 3-4 hours before the ride (optional for a ride of less than 2 hours)
- the higher the intensity of the ride, the more important the fasting interval before the event

Four minutes before and during the ride
- 45-gram candy bar at the start of the ride
- at least 60 grams of carbohydrate, solid or liquid, per hour
- 800 milliliters (a large water bottle) of liquid per hour

Four hours post-ride
- 300 grams of carbohydrate, started immediately on getting off the bike
- a liquid carbohydrate (sports drink, energy gel, soft drink) will speed absorption
- a high-carbohydrate meal is suggested the night after the ride

CHAPTER SEVEN

Nutrition for the Endurance Cyclist

I n the last chapter, we learned that nutrition for the recreational rider (2 or 3 hours, moderate pace) was more important for a comfortable post-ride day than for the ride itself. Muscle and liver glycogen stores generally provide the Calories needed by the muscles for moderate rides of several hours duration, but need to be replenished to avoid undue fatigue later in the day.

This is not the case for endurance rides of more than 3 hours, or multiple-day rides, where a complete nutritional program focuses not only on the training diet, but on the pre-ride interval and carbohydrate supplements during the ride itself. Endurance rides will definitely cause the bonk if carbohydrates are not replaced, so snacking on the bike is essential. As intensity increases above 60 percent VO2max, it is important to avoid eating in the 4-hour pre-ride interval to avoid GI distress. And with multiple-day rides, post-ride glycogen replacement begins the preparation for the next day's ride.

The Century Ride

For most cyclists a century ride (usually ridden at 50 to 80 percent VO2max). is the culmination of several months of training. Their challenge is to have a comfortable ride, avoiding the bonk and dehydration.

During the training period, the rider needs a balanced diet meeting the energy requirements of the training program. The usual distribution of Calories should approximate 60 to 70 percent carbohydrate, 10 to 15 percent protein, and 20 to 30 percent fat. As training intensifies and the total caloric replacement needs increase, the need for carbohydrate Calories will increase, while the fat and protein requirements do not change. As a result, it is not unusual for a competitive cyclist to take in 75 to 90 percent of his or her daily Calories in the form of carbohydrates.

These Calories should be eaten in at least three meals a day. If caloric requirements are high, snacking may be necessary to avoid unwanted weight loss. In addition, the daily program should be structured so that a significant percentage of the Calories are taken early in the day to anticipate the needs of the day's exercise.

Although dietary fat may be of importance for endurance activities, the body's normal stores are generally more than adequate to meet these needs. Training is the only proven way to increase free fatty acid utilization. Increasing dietary fat has no proven benefit in this area, and there has been some evidence that a high-fat diet may actually decrease endurance capacity.

Protein intake should be in the neighborhood of 40 to 70 grams per day. Increasing protein intake above these requirements will not force muscle development, and the byproduct of protein metabolism, urea, requires water for its excretion by the kidneys. As a result, high-protein diets may have a long-term negative effect on kidney function and aggravate any tendency toward dehydration.

In contrast to fats and proteins, carbohydrates can enhance bicycling performance and are important in a training program. A high-carbohydrate diet increases the amount of glycogen stored in the muscles and liver. This will increase the duration of exercise to exhaustion for the competitive event as well as having a positive effect on the entire training program.

A carbohydrate-deficient diet will result in a gradual decline in muscle glycogen (stores are not completely rebuilt after each training session) and produce a chronic state of fatigue. Failure to replenish muscle glycogen has also been associated with the development of post-exercise muscle stiffness. To avoid these problems, it is important that the total caloric expenditures be replaced each day and that at least 2,400 Calories (600 grams) be carbohydrates.

As the total body energy stores are so important to the overall success of a training program, there needs to be a close and conscious monitoring of the balance between energy expenditure and caloric intake. Daily weights provide a check on this process and should be monitored each morning before exercise. Progressive weight loss should lead to a reevaluation of the overall dietary Calorie replacement program.

Glycogen loading might be considered. Recall that this program involves three days of carbohydrate depletion followed by a high-carbohydrate diet of at least 600 grams of carbohydrate per day. This replenishes the muscle glycogen stores and takes advantage of supercompensation, or loading. Some athletes feel that the weight gain and muscle stiffness that occur with this program interferes with their performance and prefer to omit the initial exercise/depletion phase. In that case, the bicyclist will maintain a continuous high-carbohydrate diet for the entire training period as described above.

A balanced diet will meet all vitamin and mineral requirements during the training period. Any concerns about deficiencies from unusual dietary habits or a weight loss program can be allayed with the use of a daily multivitamin. Salt replacement is generally unnecessary unless fluid loss will exceed 4 percent BW (body weight).

Although simple carbohydrates should be avoided in the hour or two immediately preceding your ride, there is almost unanimous support for the benefits of a pre-ride meal of 300 grams of complex carbohydrates 3 to 4 hours before the event. These carbohydrates not only "top off" your muscle and liver glycogen stores, their slow digestion and absorption may provide an ongoing glucose supplement from your intestinal tract after the ride has started. Although claims to the contrary have been made, recent studies have demonstrated that commercial energy bars offer no performance advantages over a more traditional and less expensive complex carbohydrate such as oatmeal for this pre-ride meal.

A low residue (fiber) content and low salt content are also recommended. Because of its more rapid stomach emptying, digestion, and absorption, a liquid pre-ride meal can be used up to 2 hours prior to the ride. Liquids are preferred by some bicyclists who claim they experience less nausea with exercise than with a more solid meal.

A carbohydrate snack immediately prior to competition (5 to 10 minutes) will prolong the duration of exercise to exhaustion by protecting muscle glycogen stores in a similar manner to the supplements taken while exercising. To minimize the chance of hypoglycemia, it is important to time the consumption of this snack closely to the beginning of the event.

Carbohydrate supplements during the ride are essential. Drinks with a 10 percent glucose concentration are preferable and complex carbohydrates may give an additional edge by supplying even more carbohydrate Calories. Once fatigue has occurred, oral glucose is much less effective in prolonging high-level aerobic activities, so on the bike, carbohydrate snacks, including energy gels and sports drinks, should be started with the ride. One gram of glucose per minute (four Calories per minute, 240 Calories per hour) is easily absorbed and metabolized during exercise, and some recent research suggests that complex carbohydrate drinks may increase this to 800 Calories per hour.

Another strategy to enhance the use of muscle glucose stores includes modifying the exercise intensity (percentage VO2max), which in turn alters the balance of glucose and FFAs as energy sources for exercise. This relationship is not a linear one. That is, a 20-percent increase in percent VO2max from 50 to 70 percent will utilize less additional glucose than the increase from 70 to 90 percent. This means an endurance athlete will utilize additional fat Calories for energy or cover more miles before glycogen is depleted, by simply slowing down. This is of particular importance if a sprint might be needed at the end of the ride. As glycogen is the fuel for aerobic exercise at 100 percent VO2max and for all anaerobic activity, a bicyclist who has used all his or her glycogen is truly "out of gas."

Fluid replacement should be started 15 to 20 minutes before the start of the event. A fluid deficit of less than 2 percent BW does not appear to have an adverse effect on performance. However, with a deficit of 3 percent BW, a decrease in endurance can be demonstrated, and at 4 to 7 percent BW, there is a definite deterioration in muscle strength. There is a persistent deficit in performance for up to 4 hours after rehydration has taken place. It appears that 800 milliliters, or approximately 1 quart, is near the limit that can be emptied per hour from the stomach; as exercise intensity increases, this rate decreases, and nausea and abdominal distention can occur if larger volumes are pushed.

During severe conditions of temperature or humidity, or with prolonged training and competitive sessions, regular pre- and post-event weighing can help to assess the adequacy of fluid replacement. For rides of less than 4 hours, all weight loss can be assumed to be fluid related.

The immediate post-exercise period provides an additional opportunity for replacing muscle glycogen, and snacking during those few hours is encouraged. Post-event nutrition is particularly important if regular training is planned the next day. An ideal goal is 300 grams of carbohydrate in the 4-hour post-event period. A carbohydrate drink or an energy gel, especially a complex carbohydrate, will speed absorption and take maximal advantage of this period of increased glycogen resynthesis. And a high-carbohydrate meal that evening will continue the restocking of muscle glycogen.

Multiple-Day Rides

From a nutritional perspective, a multiple-day ride can be viewed as a series of century rides.

A solid training diet maximizes muscle and liver glycogen at the start of the trip and helps with glycogen resynthesis when off the bike. It is essential that the training diet be augmented with carbohydrate supplements during the daily rides, and close attention to the immediate 4-hour post-ride interval glycogen window is a key to maximizing glycogen stores for the next day's ride.

Recommended Nutrition Plan
Four days prior to the ride

- balanced diet meeting daily caloric needs with 60 to 70 percent of Calories as carbohydrates
- at least 600 grams of carbohydrates per day for the four days before the ride

Four hours prior to the ride

- 300-gram carbohydrate meal four hours before the ride
- the higher the intensity of the ride, the more important the fasting interval before the event

Four minutes before and during the ride

- 45-gram candy bar at the start of the ride
- at least 60 grams of carbohydrate per hour as snacks, energy gels, or sports drinks
- liquid sports drinks will provide Calories and fluids
- 800 milliliters (a large water bottle) of liquid per hour

Four hours post ride

- 300 grams of carbohydrate started immediately on getting off the bike
- a liquid carbohydrate (sports drink, energy gel, soft drink) will speed absorption
- a high-carbohydrate meal is suggested the night after the ride, especially for multi-day rides

CHAPTER EIGHT

Nutrition for the Elite Cyclist

This chapter is for those trying to get the maximum from their bodies in bicycling sports. Dedication and physical training remain the cornerstones of a program to maximize one's natural abilities. Although nutritional conditioning will never be a substitute for a demanding physical training program, a good dietary program is essential to achieving and maintaining top physical performance. Given two equally talented and trained competitors, sound nutrition will provide the additional edge that makes one a winner.

These events are high in intensity (above 90 percent VO2max) and relatively short in duration (10 to 30 miles). Muscle glycogen stores are generally adequate for the entire event, decreasing the demands for on-the-bike carbohydrate supplements, although recent research has suggested that using carbohydrate drinks may provide a slight performance edge. Fluid replacement is a basic that is too often ignored. A sound training diet maximizes glycogen stores, and post-ride glycogen replacement will minimize fatigue during ongoing training.

Track Events and Criteriums

These events require 80 to 100 percent VO2max for 1 to 2 hours; the athlete will occasionally slip into anaerobic metabolism during a sprint.

The training diet is critical in assuring that maximum glycogen stores are available at the start of the event. A major concern is chronic glycogen depletion from regular training if the daily diet fails to replace caloric expenditures. And contrary to "pop" nutritionists, it is carbohydrates, not fats or protein, that are the key to success. The four days before the ride are the time to maximize the body's glycogen reserves, and a goal should be an intake of at least 600 grams of carbohydrate per day during this period.

Muscle glycogen will generally meet the energy requirements for an event of an hour or less, but because anaerobic metabolism during a sprint is very inefficient, and requires large amounts of glycogen when compared to equal aerobic energy output, it is strongly suggested that competitors eat a 300-gram carbohydrate meal 4 hours before the competition. This is particularly so if the criterium or race will last more than an hour.

On-the-bike glucose drinks were traditionally felt to be of little use for races or events lasting less than an hour. Recent research, however, has suggested that oral glucose supplements give the rider an additional edge in events of any duration. Another benefit is fluid replacement, as dehydration is a major factor in decreased performance.

Post-event supplements are of strategic importance to replenish body glycogen stores, if one is scheduled to ride in another event the same or the following day. And even without a next-day event, they help to prepare you for your regular training schedule.

Intervals

The diet plan for interval training is similar to that for track events and criteriums. The fact that you will be consciously keeping your activity level anaerobic (greater than 100 percent VO2max) increases the importance of the 4-hour pre-event fast. It is important to have your stomach empty to minimize the risk of nausea and bloating.

Because of increased sweat losses, you will also need to pay close attention to fluid replacement.

Triathlons

A triathlon is defined as any athletic contest involving three separate events done sequentially. The first triathlon was held in San Diego in 1974. Although usually considered to be a combination of swimming, bicycling, and running, other sports can be substituted. To successfully compete, a rigorous training program is essential, and adequate nutrition is a key component of any winning strategy.

Unfortunately cross-training for triathlons is minimally effective. Although some improvement in cardiac performance carries over from one event to another, the majority of the training benefits are muscle specific, related only to the muscle group being exercised. As a result of the intense training required for the three separate events, daily caloric expenditures are high, and the time available for eating and glycogen replacement is minimized. This places an extra burden on the triathlete to avoid chronic glycogen depletion and training fatigue. A high-carbohydrate training diet matching Calories eaten to those expended is a key to maximizing training effectiveness.

Two aspects of nutrition are unique to the triathlete's training program. The first is training to eat and drink while exercising for the specific purpose of developing a tolerance for refueling during the actual competition events. The second aspect is using the 4-hour post-exercise period for rapid muscle glycogen replacement to maximize recovery and supply the energy required for several discrete training sessions per day.

During the long periods of training, the triathlete can easily lose 2 liters of fluid per hour. As thirst often lags behind the actual state of hydration, it is easy to develop a state of mild, chronic dehydration. This puts the athlete at risk of decreased performance the day of the event. This risk can be minimized by periodically checking body weights and urine-specific gravity (concentration) during the training program.

70

The nutrition recommendations for the four days and 4 hours before the competition parallel those for a century rider (see chapter 7).

During competition, the benefits of carbohydrate supplementation parallel those of other endurance activities. If the entire event will last less than 2 hours, carbohydrate supplementation is generally not needed, although fluid replacement is essential. For longer events, carbohydrate supplements are a necessity, but need tailoring to the event. For example, during the swimming leg, no eating is possible. While bicycling, solid foods can be eaten early with a transition to liquid carbohydrate supplements before the start of the run. And liquids are preferred during the run itself.

Because of the duration of some triathlons, electrolyte replacement may be prudent. Hyponatremia (a low blood sodium level) is generally not a problem in triathlons of less than 4 hours, is an occasional problem in those 4 to 8 hours long, and is a definite risk in triathlons lasting more than 8 hours. Using an average loss of 2 liters of sweat per hour, and figuring a conservative salt content one quarter that of body fluid, a goal of 1 to 2 grams of salt per hour as replacement has been suggested.

Postcompetition carbohydrate repletion again parallels that of the century rider as covered in chapter 7.

Finally, studies of micronutrient needs have suggested that triathletes, as a group, may, be at risk for isolated deficiencies. There have been reports of marginal total body zinc levels, and as many as 50 percent of triathletes may have early iron deficiency. As these minerals can have gastrointestinal as well as other toxic side effects in high doses, supplements should be taken only after discussion with a physician or trainer knowledgeable as to the pros and cons of their use.

Multi-Day Stage Races

The ultimate example of a multi-day staged road race is the Tour de France. This race is typically three weeks long, covering roughly 4,000 kilometers. The average energy intake of the participants is 5,700 Calories per day, with almost 50 percent of the Calories eaten while on the bike. More than 70 percent of the total Calories are from carbohydrates, and 30 percent of the carbohydrate Calories are from carbohydrate-rich drinks.

Studies of actual Tour participants were used to develop a laboratory model of similar exercise intensity over a six-day period. In this a model, 1,500 cc of a carbohydrate-rich solution (20 percent weight to volume, long-chain glucose polymer) was used to supplement the high-carbohydrate diet. Several interesting findings were:
1. As prolonged, intensive bicycling increased energy expenditures above 4,600 Calories per day, the athletes were unable to consume enough conventional food to replace caloric expenditures.
2. Using a concentrated carbohydrate solution did permit energy balance to be maintained.

3. Protein requirements under exercise circumstances were in excess of 1.5 grams per kilogram of body weight per day, but the use of a carbohydrate-rich diet and concentrated carbohydrate supplement to maintain energy balance decreased protein oxidation to a level requiring a protein intake of 1.5–1.8 grams of protein per kilogram of body weight per day.

In an elegant follow-up study using a similar physiological model and carbohydrate supplement, they demonstrated:

1. The use of a 20 percent complex carbohydrate drink spared intramuscular glycogen and increased exercise time to exhaustion.
2. Post-exercise use of the carbohydrate supplement permitted glycogen replacement to reach supercompensation levels within 24 hours.
3. Trained individuals had an increased lactate clearance and also an increased capacity to metabolize intramuscular fat.

Recommended Nutrition Plan

Four days prior to the ride
• balanced diet meeting daily caloric needs with 70 percent of Calories as carbohydrates
• at least 600 grams of carbohydrate per day for the 4 days before the ride

Four hours prior to the ride
• 300-gram carbohydrate meal 4 hours before the ride
• fast for 4 hours before the event

Four minutes before and during the ride
• 45-gram candy bar at the start of the ride
• 60 grams of carbohydrate per hour as an energy gel or sports drinks on the bike; glucose supplements not needed for interval training
• 800 to 1,000 milliliters of liquid per hour

Fours hours post-ride
• 300 grams of carbohydrate started immediately on getting off the bike
• a liquid carbohydrate (sports drink, energy gel, soft drink) will speed absorption
• a high-carbohydrate meal is suggested the night after the ride, especially for multi-day staged races

CHAPTER NINE

Nutrition for Mountain Biking

Although mountain biking requires unique technical skills, particularly in the area of balance, the physical and nutritional requirements are similar to those of bicyclists doing interval training or riding in a criterium (chapter 8). Nutrition is important in a training program to prevent the chronic fatigue that can occur from inadequate replacement of training Calories, and to position you for a personal best performance when riding competitively or with a group. It will not let you cut corners in your physical training program.

With the varied terrain faced on the mountain bike, from the perspective of exercise physiology, the ride is very similar to doing intervals. There are frequent periods of aerobic activity approaching 100 percent VO2max, anaerobic periods with the cells oxygen demands outstripping the available oxygen supply from the circulatory system (greater than 100 percent VO2max), and occasional downhill sections that allow the body to "regroup" for the next required burst of energy.

Generally these rides are short, and less than 2 hours. Assuming a good training diet, the pre-ride glycogen stores in the muscles should be adequate for the ride, although the more anaerobic activity, the faster this glycogen is utilized. With the high energy output, and sweating that accompanies it, fluid losses need to be considered and replaced. And the high level of exertion will decrease stomach emptying and absorption of oral supplements. These three factors make carbohydrate or sports drinks an ideal, on-the-bike approach for Calorie supplements.

Mountain Biking Diet

A good training diet assures that maximum muscle and liver glycogen stores will be available at the start of the ride. Chronic muscle glycogen depletion can occur with regular training when the daily diet doesn't replace the Calories used during training. The training diet is a key factor in success for those riding in these events of less than 2 hours duration. And it is carbohydrates, not fats or protein, that are the key to success. The training diet and four-day pre-event period present an opportunity to maximize the body's glycogen reserves, and a goal of at least 600 grams of carbohydrate per day assures that this will be achieved.

Although muscle and liver glycogen will provide all the glucose energy needed for an event of an hour or less, mountain bikers anticipating a slightly longer ride or race can benefit from a 300-gram carbohydrate meal eaten 4 hours

73

before the ride. This is particularly true as the anaerobic metabolism during short bouts of high energy output (a short hill for example) is very inefficient, and requires large amounts of glucose compared to aerobic activities. The former drains the body's reserves more quickly and makes both optimal muscle stores and oral supplements that much more important.

A carbohydrate snack immediately (5 to 10 minutes) prior to the ride has been demonstrated to prolong the duration of exercise to exhaustion, presumably by protecting muscle glycogen stores in the same manner as oral supplements eaten while exercising. Carbohydrate supplements while riding are important as well. Although glucose supplements are traditionally felt to be of little use in rides of less than an hour, recent research has suggested that carbohydrate supplements are of benefit in these events as well. Liquids with a 10 percent glucose concentration are preferable; sports drinks containing complex carbohydrates may give an additional edge by supplying even more carbohydrate Calories. It is important that carbohydrate supplements be started at the same time as the event. Once fatigue has occurred, oral glucose is much less effective in prolonging performance. During exercise, a 10 percent glucose solution supplying one gram of glucose per minute, or 60 grams (240 Calories) per hour will supplement muscle stores. And recent research work suggests that up to 800 milliliters per hour of a 20 percent to 25 percent solution (200 grams of carbohydrate) may be absorbed and metabolized.

For rides of less than an hour or two, it is usually inadequate fluid replacement rather than lack of glucose or carbohydrate supplements that are responsible for poor performance. Fluid replacement should be started on a preventive basis 15 to 20 minutes before the start of the ride, particularly in adverse conditions with high temperatures and very high, or very low, humidity. Dehydration not only affects immediate performance, but can have an affect that lasts up to 4 hours. So it isn't easy to reverse the problem of inadequate fluids after the problem has already developed. As mentioned above, at least 800 to 1,000 milliliters of fluid can be absorbed per hour. But the stomach does have its limits. As exercise intensity increases, the rate of stomach emptying decreases, and this volume of fluids may decrease as well. Nausea and abdominal distention are the risk if larger volumes of fluids are pushed. Regular pre- and post-event weights can help in assessing fluid replacement. For rides of less than 4 hours, all weight loss can be assumed to be fluid related.

Post-event carbohydrates are important to restore body glycogen in anticipation of a return to a regular training schedule, and may decrease the muscle stiffness that results from "wringing" all the glycogen out of the muscles during extreme competition. Post-ride carbohydrates are of strategic importance if one is to ride in another event on the same or the following day. As reviewed previously, the immediate post-exercise period provides an additional opportunity for replacing muscle glycogen, and snacking during those few hours is encouraged. A reasonable goal is 300 grams of carbohydrate in the 4-hour post-event period. A carbohydrate drink, especially a complex carbohydrate, will speed absorption and take advantage of this period of maximal glycogen resynthesis. And a high-carbohydrate meal that evening will continue the restocking of muscle glycogen.

Recommended Nutrition Plan

Four days prior to the ride
- balanced diet meeting daily caloric needs with 60 to 70 percent of Calories as carbohydrates
- at least 600 grams of carbohydrate per day for the 4 days before the ride

Four hours prior to the ride
- 300-gram carbohydrate meal 4 hours before the ride
- fast for 4 hours before the event to minimize abdominal bloating and distress

Four minutes before and during the ride
- 45-gram candy bar at the start of the ride
- at least 60, and as much as 200, grams of carbohydrate per hour as an energy gel or sports drinks
- 800 to 1,000 milliliters of liquid per hour

Four hours post-ride
- 300 grams of carbohydrate, started immediately on getting off the bike
- a liquid carbohydrate (sports drink, energy gel, soft drink) will speed absorption
- a high-carbohydrate meal is suggested the night after the ride

CHAPTER TEN

Carrying Your Calories

Now that you've made a decision on your fuel for the day, it's time to review the alternatives available for carrying it on your bike trip. There are several options (see figure 10.1), each with their own advantages and disadvantages. Although there are some disadvantages associated with carrying food on the bike, a little planning can minimize them.

Packaging and Packing

With commercial products packaging is rarely a problem, since durable packaging is part of successful food marketing. However, repacking foods purchased in bulk or packaging those prepared at home can be a challenge, especially with liquid or semisolid items.

In competitive events, where even small distractions can cost valuable seconds, packaging for ease of access is a major part of planning for caloric supplements. For the recreational rider, planning to eat while on the bike, safety is the issue, as even a momentary lapse in concentration can lead to a fall. And for those planning a relaxed outing with a stop to eat, packaging to prevent leaks and to maintain an appetizing appearance and presentation is the challenge.

There is no universal answer to the packaging challenge, as each food and type of event has its own unique requirements. In competitive events, where time is of the essence, less is truly more, and foods such as cookies and dried fruits that need no wrappers are favored. If the event allows a few additional seconds for eating, but still requires eating on the bike, loosely wrapped nonliquid items can be added to the menu. But beware of those prepackaged items that come in indestructible plastic and require two hands and scissors to open. For the picnic crowd, self-sealing Tupperware-type containers are best, and come in various sizes and shapes.

Once individual items have been packaged, they need to be packed for the event. For the single rider with a one-course meal, this is rarely a problem, but for larger groups and multi-course meals, some planning is necessary. The effect of vibration and shifting, or migration of containers, needs to be anticipated. This can be minimized by using your picnic accessories, such as napkins or the tablecloth, for packing material, or with alternatives such as loosely balled newspaper or foam rubber. The latter can be precut to protect not only food containers but also glassware for those planning the truly elegant outing.

Snacks

Packaging snacks is an often neglected but very important part of successful on-the-bike carbohydrate supplementation. Transportability, accessibility, and portion size need to be considered. Snacks to be consumed while riding should be in a form that is durable and will transport well until eaten. Prepare or purchase them in bite-size pieces, and package them for easy access when needed. Hard cookies, fig bars, apple slices, orange slices, and granola bars are already in an ideal size for eating on the bike.

Plastic sandwich bags make a simple packaging for snack foods that are durable but might crumble or melt in your pocket. They do not work well for multiple servings, as it is difficult to open the bag and separate the contents while continuing to concentrate on the road. For this reason, single-portion packaging is recommended for competitive riding or whenever a fast snack on the bike is planned. The ideal model for an on-the-bike snack is the trusty banana, which must have been developed by a bicyclist. It carries well in a jersey pocket, is packaged in a biodegradable wrapper, is readily accessible using one hand and the teeth, and adapts easily to single-bite portions.

Carrying Options

The jersey pocket allows the simplest, safest, and easiest access to food while riding. And it is far and away the preference of competitive riders. It has the advantage of easy accessibility with minimal effects on bike handling and aerodynamics. The disadvantage lies in the limited carrying capacity. The alternative in competitive events is the musette, or food bag, handed to the riders at predetermined locations. This is suited to long-distance events where the bulk and weight of the food needed to replace the Calories being expended would not fit in the pockets of a cycling jersey and would have a negative impact on performance if it were.

The fanny pack is gaining increased acceptance by competitive, long-distance, and recreational bikers. It has been used by cross-country skiers for years and, because it is attached by a waist belt, has the advantage of leaving the shoulders and upper body free. The weight is carried quite low and, thus, has no effect on shoulder fatigue. This pack can hold more than the pockets of a jersey, yet it can be accessed while riding if needed. Although the pack is usually worn in back to eliminate any interference when assuming the aerodynamic drop position while bicycling, it can be pulled around to the front with minimal effort while sitting in the upright position. Then, either one or both hands can be used to open the zipper and remove the food. A disadvantage is that the pack is at the same level as the jersey pockets, which eliminates their use for food storage. The cumbersome reversal of the fanny pack described above needs to be repeated each time food is removed, and in the long run it is less efficient than using a bike pack and transferring to the jersey pockets during occasional brief stops.

The handlebar bag has the advantage of being readily accessible, and, with some caution, it can be opened while moving. It does increase wind drag and can affect steering responsiveness when loaded.

There are various other bike packs available for carrying food, but all suffer from the disadvantage of being inaccessible while riding. These can carry larger quantities, are attached directly to the bike, and don't hinder riding positions or increase upper body or back fatigue. Their disadvantages include an increase in surface area and wind drag, as well as a decrease in the responsiveness and maneuverability of the bike.

Bike packs, in order of increasing capacity, include the seat bag, rack-top pack, front panniers, and rear panniers. The seat bag, or saddle bag, though not as popular in the United States as it is in Britain, is available in a wide variety of sizes. It can be quite small (holding no more than a spare inner tube and a candy bar) or large enough for a full meal. The saddle bag's position is relatively aerodynamic and has a minimal effect on bike handling and performance.

The rack-top pack carries more than does a handlebar bag and most seat bags, is slightly more aerodynamic in its location behind the rider and seat post, and has less effect on handling characteristics. It is my favorite to carry food for group outings. The rack-top pack requires a bike rack (as do panniers).

Panniers have the advantage of holding large quantities of food and other items. They do have a significant wind-drag effect and are heavy enough to influence bike handling significantly when loaded. They are available in smaller versions intended to be used on the front fork, and these can also be carried on the back rack for day trips to cut down weight and wind drag.

The traditional backpack is another possibility, but is uncomfortable on longer rides. The shoulders are a weak area for many riders, and the stress of a loaded backpack can accentuate this. For this reason, it is recommended only for short trips when no alternatives are readily available.

The ultimate pack is the sagwagon, a car or van following the bicyclists. It allows almost unlimited carrying capacity, including the bike and rider if all is not going well. It represents the ultimate in rider comfort as no additional weight needs to be carried on the bike or by the rider. And it is readily accessible, even providing the option of obtaining food while moving in the form of a quick hand-off. Its major disadvantage is a philosophical one for those bicyclists who wish to be truly self-propelled. For mountain biking, the sagwagon is of more limited use, as it cannot follow the riders but must meet up with them when they return to civilization.

Carrying Fluids

Unlike solid foods, there are limited options for carrying fluids. All require a closed container, usually a plastic bottle which is carried on the bike in a cage or rack. This water bottle cage is attached to either the down tube or the seat tube, but can also be attached to the handlebar stem for easier access, or behind the seat itself if additional carrying capacity is desired. On occasion, the water bottle can be carried in a jersey pocket, again when an additional or reserve bottle is desired. It should be carried in the middle pocket of the traditional three-pocket jersey to minimize the tendency to slide to either side.

The traditional water bottle spigot is a nipple with a slide closure which drains directly from the top of the bottle. This requires the bottle and head to be tipped while drinking, with the attendant risk of getting a mouthful of air and water when the bottle is partially empty and not tipped quite far enough. A greater danger lies in the need to take your eyes off the road while drinking this way. A major advance has been the use of a drain tube extending to the bottom of the bottle, which eliminates the need to tip the bottle to drink and eliminates the air surge from an almost empty bottle. The initial design has been refined with the addition of a hand bulb pump and extension tubing to allow the bottle to remain in the cage, while manual air pressurization delivers fluid directly into the mouth.

And with the increased emphasis on hydration and demand for easy use in off-road cycling, which requires that both hands be on the handlebars at all times, we have seen the ultimate refinement of the fluid delivery system. A fluid bladder contained in a backpack, carried on the bicyclist's back, uses gravity to deliver fluid through a plastic tube directly to the biker's mouth. This is the ultimate in safety and ease of use, providing the increased fluids needed by competitive mountain bikers who have minimal ground support or access to refill traditional water bottles.

Figure 10.1 Comparison of Carrying Options

Option	Carrying Capacity	Rider Comfort	Access	Air Drag	Bike Handling
Jersey pocket	+	-	++++	ME	ME
Backpack	+++	-	0	ME	-
Fanny pack	++	-	++	ME	ME
Seat pack	++	ME	0	-	ME
Handlebar bag	++	ME	+	-	-
Rack pack	+++	ME	0	-	-
Panniers	++++	ME	0	-	-

Legend

ME = minimal effect   - = relatively worse

+ = relatively better   0 = not applicable

CHAPTER ELEVEN

Where to Eat

Now that we have decided what to eat and how we are going to carry the food on the bike, let's consider the options of where to eat. Evolution has adapted humans to be able to eat in all positions and under almost all conditions. Since this book was written to increase the enjoyment of cycling, here are a few tips to liven up your tour or ride.

Eating on the Bike

The most common place to eat while cycling is, you guessed it, on the bike. This goes for the recreational cyclist as well as the competitive rider. A major consideration is safety.

Eating while on the bike takes some practice and concentration. A mouthful of food can affect the rhythm of your breathing and can easily be aspirated into the windpipe. Keep the following tips in mind to avoid unnecessary risks:

1. Slow down.
2. Increase your concentration on the road, anticipating upcoming obstacles or hazards.
3. In a pace line, eat at the end, not in the middle or while pulling.
4. On hilly terrain, eat after you crest the hill, not while climbing.
5. Keep your food in the outside back pocket of your jersey.
6. Drink from your downtube bottle until it's empty and then switch with your full seat tube bottle.

Roadside Shops

Bakeries are the second most common eating spots. Seasoned tourers will often use a bakery as an intermediate goal to break up the tedium of a long ride. It is helpful to space these bakery stops at 2-hour intervals, when muscle glycogen stores are usually approaching exhaustion and need replenishing. A good tour or ride leader will often scout out the best bakeries and plan the day accordingly. These stops minimize the need to carry extra weight and bulk on the bike. In fact, it is the availability of bakeries and the associated opportunity to carbo replete en route that provide the major incentive for many Saturday riders.

The use of bed and breakfast, or B&B, accommodations is an extension of the bakery concept for the multiple-day tour. These stops provide comfortable lodgings and a pleasant breakfast before heading off for the first bakery. They minimize the need to carry camping gear and can provide a goal for the tour if they are in a unique setting. As with bakeries, the wise tour leader will often plan the trip around the most desirable B&Bs, knowing that the psychological diversion of the evening will often make the next day's riding that much more pleasant.

Sagwagon

When a sagwagon is used, particularly when the driver is someone who wants to participate in the group camaraderie but either can't or does not want to ride, a modification of the B&B approach is very successful. In this case, the bicyclists set off after deciding on a predetermined meeting point for the midday meal break. The sagwagon driver then has the option of sleeping in, lounging around, or reconnoitering the local gift shops before setting out in the morning.

The sagwagon carries the food and whatever else is needed for a major midday meal, ranging from a simple picnic to a regal affair with all the trimmings, including real plates, flatware, and glasses. After a relaxed lunch, the driver proceeds to the night's lodging and again has extra time to relax or take a short ride before the bike group arrives. This approach opens up many options for bicycling families, particularly when there are divergent goals and abilities. The fact that a motor vehicle is available also extends the possibilities for the evening meal.

Picnic Spots

The ultimate challenge is often picking an appropriate spot for your picnic, whether supported by a sagwagon or when carrying the meal entirely on the bike. Fortunately, there are limitless possibilities. While bakeries are in predetermined locations, a picnic can be set almost anywhere. A quiet spot off the highway is preferable, and additional rustic trappings, such as a stream or a lake, can add to the atmosphere.

Most people have their own mental image of the ideal setting for a picnic, and with the miles of country roads and off-road terrain now accessible by mountain bike, you will find many superb spots along your way or just a little off the beaten track. It is the multitude of possibilities that makes bike tours and the picnics that go along with them so appealing to the adventuresome.

CHAPTER TWELVE

Practical Tips

In previous chapters we applied the basics of exercise physiology and nutrition to develop a nutritional training program for bicyclists. Next we reviewed issues related to packaging and transporting that food on the bike. In this chapter, we'll review road-tested practical tips from bicyclists to help you tailor a bicycling nutrition plan to your specific needs.

Snacks and Light Meals

Foods in this category form the backbone of any serious cycling program, providing variety and an occasional psychological lift for those out on a pleasure ride. The difference between a snack and a light meal is often difficult to define, but hinges on the factors of quantity and quality, such as:

1. How much is eaten at any one time?
2. Do you want to eat on the bike or stop to do so?

The philosophy of food breaks varies with one's goals. Recreational riders with the luxury of time will stop to enjoy their snacks, while those in a competitive mode will begin snacking on the bike early in the ride in anticipation of the delay in stomach emptying that occurs with strenuous exercise. Any Calories absorbed will delay glycogen depletion and the onset of fatigue, or the bonk.

The secret for maximum performance in events that last more than 2 hours (the time at which muscle glycogen depletion occurs) is to snack frequently, at least every 20 to 30 minutes. A successful program requires a compromise between eating enough to prevent hunger and avoiding the pitfall of "if a little is good, a lot must be better," with the risk of stomach distention, bloating and nausea, and a deterioration in performance.

The first step in planning a program of on-the-bike snacks is to estimate your caloric requirements per hour. Next, choose a schedule for snacking that meets your riding style; every 15 or 20 minutes is a practical compromise. Then, using the suggestions below, a specific program can be tailored to meet your needs. The final step is a road test. This is a key point, as physiologic and digestive functions vary from person to person and may require individual refinements to meet your specific needs or preferences.

Foods in this section can also be used in the pre-race meal. If a vigorous ride is planned, they should be eaten at least 4 hours prior to the start of the event. This assures that your stomach will be empty and that the bulk of digestion and absorption will have occurred before the inevitable slow-down that comes with exercise.

Snack Survey

A survey of favorite snack foods revealed some common favorites and some refreshing individuality as well. Dried fruits were the most common choice for on-the-bike snacks, probably related to their high caloric content, the ease of preparing bite-size portions, and their relative indestructibility in a jersey pocket on a long ride. Complex carbohydrates, such as baked potatoes, were also near the top of the list. Figure 12.1 summarizes the results of this survey and includes the Calories per average serving. For perspective, remember that at 15 miles per hour a 165-pound rider expends approximately 400 Calories per hour.

Two prepared delicacies hold promise, but the exact caloric content could not be determined due to individual variation in preparation. The first was a sandwich of jelly and cream cheese. The second, a mixture of peaches, honey, and water in a plastic bag, reinforces that there is plenty of room for experimentation in the snack area.

Another option is the commercial powerbars or sports bars. Although they are advertised as providing a particularly potent combination of ingredients, these bars are no more effective on a gram-for-gram basis as an energy booster than other carbohydrate snacks. Their advantages include the fact that they are prepackaged, are readily available commercially, and offer another taste and texture option.

Occasionally, you are caught out on the bike when the munchies or the bonk hits. There are a lot of enticing items at the 7-11, but you want to pick something that is low in fat and high in carbohydrates to give you a quick energy boost. Here are some thoughts:

Fruit-Flavored Yogurt: Pick the low-fat variety
•1 cup = 250 Cal, 45 grams carbo, 10 grams protein, and 2.5 grams fat

Fig bars: The old standby
•2 bars = 140 Cal, 32 grams carbo, and virtually no fat

Fruit: Almost 100 percent carbo
•1 banana = 100 Cal; 1 apple = 80 Cal; 1 orange = 60 Cal

Corn nuts: Also satisfies salt craving
•2 ounces = 130 Cal, 20 grams carbo, but 4 grams (28 percent) fat

PRACTICAL TIPS

Milky Way Lite bar
• 1.5-ounce bar = 160 Cal, 33 grams carbo, and 5 grams (28 percent) fat (about half that found in most candy bars)

There are some foods to be avoided (or at least left to the end of your experimental list). The stress of vigorous exercise can stimulate the colon, and the more vigorous the exercise (or more out of shape the rider), the greater this effect. Certain foods such as dairy products and spicy, greasy, or oily foods can accentuate this normal elimination reflex.

Moderation is the key to success in snack planning. The best advice is to start off with small amounts of those foods that sound appealing, and use your own individual response to determine their place in your nutrition program. Additional suggestions for snack foods can be found in chapter 14.

Beverages
It is safe to say that the single, biggest mistake of competitive athletes as a group is the failure to replace the fluid losses associated with exercise. This is more common in bicycling, as rapid skin evaporation decreases our awareness of perspiring and leads to a false sense of minimal fluid loss.

For a successful ride, it is essential that fluid replacement start early and continue on a regular basis.

During vigorous exercise, the sensation of thirst lags well behind fluid replacement needs. Once you notice that you are thirsty there will already be a significant fluid deficit to overcome. On a hot day, drink a minimum of four to five ounces of fluid every 15 minutes, beginning at the start of exercise. A practical way to determine if you are taking adequate fluid replacement is to weigh yourself before and after a long ride. A drop of a pound or two won't impair performance, but greater weight loss indicates the need to change your replacement routine. As you customize a fluid replacement program for your personal needs, remember that a pint of liquid weighs roughly one pound.

Several factors will modify your fluid requirements. An obvious one is the day's temperature. Another is the fluid content of your snacks. Fresh fruits, such as oranges, apples, grapes, or peaches, contain water. When used as snacks, fluid intake can be scaled back accordingly. Alcoholic beverages should be strictly avoided. Alcohol is not only a mild diuretic causing increased loss of water through the kidneys and accentuating the tendency to dehydrate, but also interferes with performance through its negative effect on glucose metabolism in the liver.

Any sugar in the replacement fluids is a bonus for the cyclist. Liquids with a 10 percent sugar concentration are readily emptied from the stomach, and any sugar is quickly absorbed and transported in the bloodstream to the muscles where it is used as an alternative to muscle glycogen stores for muscle energy needs. Drinks containing glucose polymers will provide additional Calories per ounce of fluid at the same concentration. There have been no studies confirming benefits of fruit drinks containing the sugar fructose over glucose drinks, and taste alone appears to be their advantage.

In summary, drinking plain water at a rate of 1 quart per hour is adequate for rides of 1 to 2 hours. On longer rides, where the body's glycogen stores will be approaching exhaustion, glucose supplements assume increased importance. An 8 to 10 percent sugar concentration is ideal. Glucose polymers offer the advantage of increasing the number of Calories per quart without an unpalatable sweet taste. The old standbys such as apple juice and cola drinks have the magic maximum concentration of 10 percent and are an economical alternative to the multiple sports drinks available. And studies of the rate of gastric emptying with carbonated drinks have failed to demonstrate any difference in the gastric emptying rates of water versus carbonated carbohydrates.

The physiological benefits, if any, of glucose polymers over simple sugars in replacement drinks are still being clarified. Although there is little question that more Calories can be ingested per quart of fluid, there has not been a clear performance advantage in controlled, scientific studies.

At this time, the major benefit of these polymers appears to be the absence of the sweet taste and nauseating properties that might limit overall fluid replacement.

Picnic and Gourmet Foods

Foods in this category (recipes ideas are in chapter 14) will be of interest to recreational bicyclists, particularly those who bike to eat. This group appreciates the rewards that go with maintaining fitness and replacing the Calories burned with aerobic exercise. Some of these foods can also be used for endurance rides, particularly if taste fatigue develops for the "same old foods." Be warned, however, that the higher fat content in some recipes makes them not only heavy to carry on the bike for a long trip, but may also create the same heavy sensation in the stomach.

The picnic ride can be a gala social occasion when compared to training sessions and competitive bicycling. This is a ride that appeals to the whole family and friends who only occasionally ride a bike. To the noncyclist, the picnic is the main focus, while the bicycling itself is merely an excuse for the outing. As an additional benefit, the modest ride will stimulate the appetite and enhance the taste of the meal that follows.

Packaging can be a major problem for the picnic bicyclist. It is often easier to bring the raw materials and create the finished product on site, rather than to attempt transporting the completed dish. The best results are obtained if one keeps an open and innovative mind and uses self-sealing containers that approximate the size and shape of the food being prepared. If all else fails, remember that every meal on a picnic trip tastes like gourmet fare, even if it's a little lopsided.

Bacterial growth and food poisoning can be a problem with some foods if they are not prepared and handled properly. This is especially the case with dairy products, poultry, eggs, fish, mayonnaise, and cream-filled pastries. This risk is minimized by following several simple steps. First, by preparing the food properly and using clean utensils and fresh ingredients, the chances of bacterial contamination are reduced. The second line of defense is complete cooking, which kills any bacteria that may be present. Finally, keeping the food cool after preparation slows down the growth of any bacteria that have escaped the initial two steps. It is essential to keep your prepared foods refrigerated until the last possible minute and, if possible, to use insulated Styrofoam containers for transportation to help keep them cool. Even with these precautions, it is best to eat prepared foods within 4 to 6 hours of preparation or removal from refrigeration.

Picnic Types

There are three alternatives for the bicycling picnic: the spontaneous picnic, the brown bag picnic, and the elegant picnic. The spontaneous, or minimalist, approach emphasizes off-the-shelf foods, and can be put together in any supermarket or grocery store. It includes such ready-to-eat items as cheese, nuts, crackers, bread, canned pâté, marinated mushrooms or artichokes, fruits, vegetables, and dips.

The brown bag picnic is centered on a sandwich of fresh bread and sliced meats assembled at the picnic site. For an extra touch, a salad can be easily prepared, with the dressing added later to help keep it fresh. While this picnic can be planned walking the aisles of the supermarket, it is of immeasurable help to have access to a good delicatessen.

Finally, there is the elegant, or gourmet, picnic. This is the epitome of bicycling picnics and does require prior planning and preparation time in the kitchen. Of course, any ingredients mentioned above for the spontaneous picnic can be included as well.

To aid in preparing the menu, whether minimalist or gourmet, think of the picnic as being divided into four courses. These include:

1. appetizer or soup
2. main course
3. dessert
4. beverage

If you have an item in mind for each course, you're on your way to a successful picnic.

After the food has been prepared or purchased, and the group is ready to set off for the memorable event, be sure to consult a final checklist. This is a key to successful picnic planning and has saved many an outing (and friendship). The following checklist covers the necessities:

1. tablecloth or ground cloth
2. utensils, plates, and glasses or cups
3. bottle opener (or corkscrew)
4. thermos (or ice) for cold drinks
5. sharp knife
6. light cutting board or serving platter
7. napkins, paper towels (or washcloth in Ziploc bag)
8. candles, matches
9. trash bag
10. insect repellent, suntan cream (or, where the climate dictates it, rain shelter)

Now that you have all the ingredients together, you're on your way to a pleasant part of biking that's often overlooked: the bicycle picnic. Enjoy!

International Travel

International travel presents two unique challenges. The first is finding foods both high in carbohydrate and compatible with the bicyclist's digestive tract. Fortunately, carbohydrates are the mainstay of nutrition in third world countries and are found in many forms and dishes. A sense of adventure is all that is needed. Exploring the local foods and spices in foreign lands is part of the adventure of international travel, but these interesting dishes can occasionally lead to GI distress.

A second concern relates to the possibility of traveler's diarrhea (food poisoning, tourista, Montezuma's revenge) from a bacterial infection. Again, common sense goes a long way to minimizing the risks. Eat in established restaurants rather than purchasing from street vendors, and either disinfect your own water or use bottled water if there is any question as to sterility.

As even a minor case of diarrhea can be devastating when you are depending on your own legs to get you through the day, you may wish to talk to your doctor about preventive antibiotics, particularly if you are traveling in a third world country. There are two recommended approaches. The favored is to use two Pepto Bismol tablets four times a day for prevention, and to carry a supply of an antibiotic to be started if diarrhea should occur. The other, to be considered if the risks are extremely high and the planned trip will be shorter than two weeks, is to take an

PRACTICAL TIPS

antibiotic such as doxycycline or trimethoprim sulfa daily on a preventative basis for the duration of the trip. There are pros and cons to each approach, and your physician should be able to give you further advice.

Figure 12.1 Preferred Bicycle Snacks

Food	Quantity	Calories	Carbs (gms)
Cookies			
generic	2 small	105	15
Fig Newton	1	50	20
Chips Ahoy	1	65	9
Oreo	1	47	7
graham cracker	1	30	5
animal cracker	1	30	6
ginger snap	1	30	6
vanilla wafer	1	19	3
Fresh fruit			
banana (avg)	4 oz	100	26
pear	4 oz	98	25
grapes	1 cup	57	16
orange	4 oz	65	16
apple	4 oz	80	21
peach	4 oz	37	10
cantaloupe	1 cup	57	13

Food	Quantity	Calories	Carbs (gms)
Dried fruit			
raisins	1/3 cup	150	40
apricots	10 halves	83	22
prunes	5 whole	100	53
apples	1/4 cup	52	13
figs	5 whole	238	61
fruit roll-up	1/2 oz	50	12
Candy bar	1 oz	130	16
Gum drop	1 oz	98	25
Baked potato	avg size	220	51
Pastries			
doughnut	avg size	125	14
eclair	avg size	239	23
muffin	avg size	126	20
toast	1 slice	64	11
plain bagel	1	163	31
Rice pudding	1/2 cup	193	35
Rice (cooked)	1 cup	223	50
Yogurt	1 cup	140	15

CHAPTER THIRTEEN

Training Diet

The training diet has been addressed earlier in general terms. A diet deficient in carbohydrates will result in a gradual decline in muscle glycogen, a decrease in performance, and possibly a chronic state of fatigue. It is important that total caloric expenditures be replaced each day.

Most athletes focus their energy on the physical aspects of a training program and spend little time on their meal menus. As a result, it is a challenge for them to maintain a balanced, high-carbohydrate diet during the training period. This chapter provides a practical approach to this problem.

During training it is important to eat a wide variety of foods to maximize nutrition and take advantage of the micronutrients that may be missed by eating the same foods every day. Rice, pasta, grains, and beans, along with a variety of fresh fruits and vegetables, form the center of the meal, while meat and desserts play a supporting role.

Although pasta has a reputation as the carbohydrate of choice for athletes, rice at 23 grams of carbohydrate per 1/2 cup, packs more complex carbohydrate than pasta with 20 grams of carbo per 1/2 cup serving, or potatoes at 15 grams per 1/2 cup. Plus rice can be blended with milk and eggs to make a Calorie-dense pudding that some bicyclists carry in plastic bags for a quick snack on the bike, and at four cents per 1/2 cup serving, the price is right. Other advantages of rice include the fact it is cholesterol-free, readily digestible, and gluten-free, which means that it is an alternative for those who are wheat-intolerant.

The menu in figure 13.1 is an example of a single day in a good basic training diet, providing 2,000 Calories with 60 percent from carbohydrates. The menu can be modified for individual tastes by substituting items from the "exchange" groups listed in figure 13.2. For example, if you wanted to eliminate the "3/4 cup cold cereal with 1/2 cup milk" (breakfast item, figure 13.1), you could substitute 1/2 of an English muffin (bread/starch exchange groups) and 1/2 cup of yogurt (milk exchange group) without affecting the overall nutritional or Caloric content of the day's diet.

Another option is building your own training diet from scratch using the appropriate number of recommended servings of each exchange group from figure 13.3 (to maintain the proper nutritional balance for the day) and selecting specific items for each exchange group serving (all equivalent in nutritional content) from the list in figure 13.2.

Figure 13.1 Sample 2,000-Calorie Diet

Breakfast

3/4 cup orange juice

3/4 cup cold cereal (unsweetened) with 1/2 cup milk

2 slices whole grain toast

1 teaspoon margarine or butter or preserves

1/2 cup lowfat yogurt with 3/4 cup sliced strawberries

Lunch

2 ounces shaved turkey

2 slices whole grain bread

1 tablespoon mayonnaise

lettuce

3 slices tomato

1 1/2 cup mixed fruit salad or 1 whole banana, apple, or orange

3 ginger snap cookies

1 cup milk

Dinner

1 1/2 cup spaghetti with 1 cup meat sauce

1 tablespoon Parmesan

1 slice Italian bread

1 teaspoon margarine or olive oil

2 cups tossed salad

2 tablespoons low-Calorie dressing or a sprinkle of raspberry vinegar and a grind of black pepper

Snack 1

1/2 cup frozen yogurt or iced milk with 3/4 cup sliced peaches

Snack 2

3 cups air-popped popcorn

Snack 3

1 small orange

Figure 13.2 Exchange Groups
Starch/bread

1/2 cup pasta or barley

1/3 cup cooked rice or cooked beans

1 small potato (or 1/2 cup mashed)

1/2 cup corn, peas, or squash

1 slice bread or 1 roll

1/2 English muffin, bagel, or hamburger/hot dog bun

1/2 cup cooked cereal

3/4 cup dried cereal (unsweetened)

5 crackers

3 cups popcorn, unbuttered and air-popped

Meat

1 ounce lean, skinless poultry, fish, or meat

1 chicken leg = 2 ounces

1 small pork chop = 3 ounces

1 small hamburger = 3 ounces

1 medium fish fillet = 3 ounces

1/4 cup cottage cheese

1/4 cup canned salmon or tuna

1 tablespoon peanut butter

1 egg

1 ounce low-fat cheese

Vegetable

1 cup raw vegetables
1/2 cup tomato juice or vegetable juice

Fruit

1 fresh medium fruit
1 cup berries or melon
1/2 cup canned fruit in juice without sugar
1/2 cup fruit juice
1/4 cup dried fruit

Milk

1 cup skimmed milk
1 cup plain lowfat yogurt

Figure 13.3 Exchange Group Nutritional Content

Exchange Groups	Carb (gm)	Protein (gm)	Fat (gm)	Cal	No. of Servings in 2,000-Calorie Diet
Starch/bread	15	3	trace	80	12
Meat (lean)	-	7	5	75	4
Vegetable	5	2	-	25	4
Fruit	15	-	-	60	6
Milk (skim)	12	8	trace	90	2

CHAPTER FOURTEEN

Recipes

In this final chapter, you will find a collection of recipes that are particularly suit-able for bicycling snacks, drinks, and picnics.

The recipes marked with asterisks (*) are those that can be prepared easily away from home, while the others require more extensive preparation in the kitchen.

Snacks

George's Bars

1/4 pound margarine or butter

4 eggs, beaten

1 cup flour (optional: 1/2 as whole wheat flour)

1/2 teaspoon baking powder

1 teaspoon salt

1 3/4 cup sugar (optional: 1/2 as brown sugar)

2 cups dates (or raisins, other dried fruits)

2 1/2 cups chopped walnuts

3 tablespoons molasses (optional)

Preheat oven to 350 degrees Fahrenheit. Melt butter and cool slightly. Add eggs. Sift together flour, baking powder, salt, and sugar and add to eggs/shortening mix. Combine fruits and nuts with batter. Spread approximately 1-inch thick in 2 greased pans. Bake 30 minutes. Cool, cut into bars.

Crispie Treats

1/4 cup margarine or butter

10-ounce package (about 40) regular marshmallows

6 cups toasted rice cereal

1 cup raisins or dried fruit (optional)

1/2 cup peanuts or other nuts (optional)

Melt butter or margarine in large saucepan over low heat. Add marshmallows and stir until completely melted. Remove from heat. Add cereal. Stir until well-coat-ed. Using buttered spatula, press mixture into 13x9x2-inch pan. Cut when cool.

Power Balls
1 cup graham cracker crumbs
1 cup toasted rice cereal
1/2 cup uncooked oatmeal (optional)
raisins, carob chips, nuts (optional)
peanut butter (room temperature)

Mix all ingredients except peanut butter in food processor. Add peanut butter until it forms a ball. Hand form to desired size and shape.

Homemade Power Bar #1
1 cup regular rolled oats
1/2 cup sesame seeds
1 1/2 cups dried apricots, finely chopped
1 1/2 cups raisins
1 cup shredded, unsweetened dry coconut
1 cup blanched almonds, chopped
1/2 cup nonfat dry milk
1/2 cup toasted wheat germ
2 teaspoons butter or margarine
1 cup light corn syrup
3/4 cup sugar
1 1/4 cups chunky-style peanut butter
1 teaspoon orange extract
2 teaspoons grated orange peel
1 package (12 ounces) or 2 cups semisweet chocolate baking chips
3/4 cup (3/4 pound) butter or margarine

Spread oats in a 10x15-inch baking pan. Bake in a 300-degree-Fahrenheit oven until oats are toasted, about 25 minutes. Stir frequently. Toast sesame seeds in a 10- to 12-inch frying pan over medium heat, about 7 minutes. Pour into a large bowl and add apricots, raisins, coconut, almonds, dry milk, and wheat germ. Mix hot oats into dried fruit mixture. Butter a hot baking pan and set aside. In a frying pan, combine corn syrup and sugar; bring to a rolling boil over medium high heat and quickly stir in the peanut butter, orange extract, and orange peel. Pour over the oatmeal mixture and mix well. Spread in buttered pan and press into an even layer. Cover and chill until firm, at least 4 hours. Cut into bars about 1 1/4x2 1/2 inches. Combine chocolate chips and butter/margarine in the top of a double boiler. Place over simmering water until melted. Stir often. Turn heat to low. Using tongs, dip 1 bar at a time into chocolate and hold over pan until it stops dripping. Place on wire racks set above waxed paper. When firm and cool (bars with butter in the chocolate coating may need to be chilled), wrap individually in foil. Store in the refrigerator up to 4 weeks or freeze to store longer.

Homemade Power Bar #2

You will note that there are no dairy products in this recipe, for those intolerant to them. You could easily replace the soy milk powder with the cow equivalent, but then you'd definitely have to include some maltodextrin (soy drink already has some in it). You could also replace about half the honey with maltodextrin if you have a local source. If you prefer cocoa to carob, you can easily substitute it.

1 cup oat bran
1/2 cup toasted sunflower and/or sesame seeds, ground using a food processor
1/2 cup soy milk powder (the soy milk powder used here has 37 percent maltodextrin, ~20 percent dextrose)
1/2 cup raisins
2 tablespoons carob powder

Mix well and add to:

1/2 cup brown rice, cooked and minced (use a food processor again)
1/2 cup peanut butter (more or less, depending on consistency)
1/2 cup honey (you may need to warm it if it's thicker)

Stir and knead until thoroughly mixed. A cake mixer works well for this. The bars can be reasonably soft, so a night in the fridge helps to bind it all together. Roll or press out about 1 cm thick and cut.

Muffins

Muffins may come closest to the ideal cycling snack. They are high in carbohydrates and allow you to add, subtract, or substitute ingredients to meet individual tastes. In addition, they are easy to carry and are an ideal single-portion size.

Oatmeal Raisin Muffins
1 1/2 cups flour (whole wheat if desired)
1 cup uncooked oatmeal
1 tablespoon baking powder
3 tablespoons sugar (or 2 tablespoons honey)

1/2 cup raisins (or other dried fruit)
1/4 cup walnuts (optional)
1 egg (or 2 egg whites)
1 cup milk
1/4 cup vegetable oil (or 1/2 stick melted margarine)

Preheat oven to 400 degrees Fahrenheit. Combine flour, oatmeal, baking powder, sugar, fruit, nuts. In a separate bowl, beat egg, then stir in milk and oil. Add liquid mixture to flour and stir until coarsely blended. Pour into 12-muffin tin lined with paper. Bake 15 to 20 minutes.

Carrot Muffins
1 1/2 cups flour (whole wheat if desired)
1/2 cup uncooked oatmeal
1/2 cup brown sugar
1 tablespoon baking powder
1 cup carrots, finely shredded
1/4 cup nuts (walnuts, sunflower seeds)
2 eggs
1/4 cup vegetable oil (or 1/2 stick melted margarine)
1/4 cup milk

Preheat oven to 400 degrees Fahrenheit. Combine flour, oatmeal, brown sugar, and baking powder. Add carrots and nuts. In a separate bowl, beat eggs, then stir in oil and milk. Add liquid mixture to flour and stir until coarsely blended. Pour into 12-muffin tin lined with paper. Bake 15 to 20 minutes.

Apple Muffins
2 cups flour (whole wheat if desired)
1 teaspoon cinnamon
1 tablespoon baking powder
1 egg (or 2 egg whites)
1/4 cup honey (or 1/2 cup brown sugar)
3/4 cup milk
1/4 cup vegetable oil (or 1/2 stick melted margarine)
1 cup shredded apple

Preheat oven to 400 degrees Fahrenheit. Combine flour, cinnamon, and baking powder. In a separate bowl, beat egg, then stir in honey, milk, oil, and apples. Add

97

liquid mixture to flour and stir until coarsely blended. Pour into 12-muffin tin lined with paper. Bake 15 to 20 minutes.

Apple Caramel Rolls
   For those with more of a sweet tooth, these caramel rolls should fill the bill. The caramel frosting makes them a challenge to eat while on the bike.

3/4 cup packed brown sugar
1/2 cup + 2 tablespoons softened margarine
36 pecan halves
2 cups Bisquick baking mix
1/2 cup cold water
1 cup finely chopped apple

   Preheat oven to 450 degrees Fahrenheit. Place 2 teaspoons brown sugar, 2 teaspoons margarine, and 3 pecan halves in each of 12 muffin cups. Melt in oven. Combine baking mix and water until soft dough forms, then beat vigorously for 20 strokes. Smooth dough into a ball on floured board. Knead 5 times. Roll dough into a rectangle (approx. 15x9 inches). Spread 2 tablespoons margarine, 1/4 cup brown sugar, and apple on the rectangle of dough. Roll up tightly. Cut into 12 1 1/4-inch-wide slices. Place slices, cut side down, in muffin cups. Bake 10 minutes. Invert immediately on a heatproof serving plate.

Beverages
   In addition to natural fruit juices, there are many ready-made commercial drinks. Two easy to prepare fluid favorites are the following:

Kool-Aid
   Add 1/4 of the amount of sugar suggested on the package instructions and up to 1/4 teaspoon salt per quart.

Tea
   Use any regular green, black, spiced, or herb tea.
   Sweeten to taste with up to 1/4 cup sugar per quart.

Shakes and Smoothies
   These provide not only fluid replacement but are also high in carbohydrate Calories. Being semiliquid, they are readily emptied from the stomach and provide a pleasant-tasting energy boost on a long ride. Two examples are:

Cathy's Banana Shake
1/2 cup orange juice
1/2 cup pineapple juice
touch of honey
2 bananas

Blend on high

Chris' Fruit Frosty*
cranberry juice
orange juice
strawberries
pineapple chunks
bananas
frozen fruit bars (grape or strawberry)
ice cubes

Blend on high

Appetizers and Soups

Gazpacho
3 large ripe tomatoes
1 red pepper
1 medium yellow onion
1 large shallot
1 large cucumber
1/4 cup red wine vinegar
1/4 cup olive oil
3/4 cup canned tomato juice
1 egg, lightly beaten
cayenne pepper, salt, black pepper
1/4 cup chopped fresh dill

Wash, core, and coarsely chop vegetables. Seed cucumber. Mix vinegar, olive oil, canned tomato juice, and egg. Using a blender or food processor, puree vegetables. Add vinegar mixture. Add cayenne, black pepper, and salt to taste. Chill. Serves 4.

RECIPES

Vichyssoise
3 tablespoons unsalted butter
4 large leeks, whites only, thinly sliced
1 small yellow onion, thinly sliced
4 potatoes, peeled and thinly sliced
3 cups chicken stock
3/4 tablespoon lemon juice
1 1/2 cup milk
2 cups whipping cream
pepper and salt

Melt butter and sauté leeks and onion. Add potatoes, chicken stock, and lemon juice. Boil for 1 hour. Cool. Process in food processor or blender. Return to pot. Add milk and one half of the cream. Season to taste with pepper and salt. Bring to a simmer for 1 minute. Remove from heat, cool, and then refrigerate. Add remaining cream just prior to serving. Serves 6.

Lemon Soup
8 cups chicken broth
4 eggs
juice of 2 lemons
salt and pepper

Heat broth. Simmer 20 minutes. Beat eggs and lemon juice together until well-blended. Slowly pour into broth while stirring. Do not boil. Heat until thickened. Do not boil. Season to taste. Chill and serve. Serves 8.

Richard's Pâté
1 large onion
1 stick celery
1/2 teaspoon garlic, crushed
3/4 pound chicken livers
1/2 pound white meat of chicken
1/4 cup walnuts, toasted
1/4 cup raisins
2 teaspoons pâté spice (see next recipe)
2 tablespoons Madeira
2 tablespoons cognac
1/4 pound unsalted butter

Grate onion and celery in food processor. Sauté onion, celery, and garlic with one-third of the butter. Return to the food processor (use steel blade). Sauté chicken livers with one-third of the butter and add to food processor. Saut≥ white meat of chicken. Add to food processor. Add walnuts, raisins, pâté, spice, Madeira, cognac, and remainder of butter to the food processor. Blend until coarsely mixed, place in pâté pan. Refrigerate. Serve with French baguettes (crusty bread) and unsalted butter. Cornichons (small French pickles) add a nice extra touch. Serves 8 to 12 as an appetizer, 4 to 6 as a light meal.

Pâté Spice (for preceding recipe)
1 teaspoon bay leaves
1 1/2 teaspoon thyme
1 1/2 teaspoon rosemary
1 1/2 teaspoon basil
2 1/2 teaspoon cinnamon
1 1/2 teaspoon mace
3/4 teaspoon ground cloves
1/4 teaspoon allspice
1/2 teaspoon ground white pepper
1 teaspoon paprika

Mix herbs and finely crush them in a spice mortar. Sift through fine sieve. Add powdered spices. Store in a tightly closed jar.

Salads

Mushroom Salad with Mustard Vinaigrette
1/4 cup Dijon style mustard
1/4 cup wine vinegar
1/2 teaspoon dried oregano, crushed
1/4 teaspoon salt
1/4 teaspoon pepper
1/2 cup olive oil or salad oil
12 ounces (4 1/2 cups) fresh mushrooms, sliced
1/2 cup pitted olives, halved

Combine mustard, vinegar, oregano, salt, and pepper in a large bowl. Using a whisk, blend in oil. Stir in mushrooms and olives. Cover and chill at least 2 hours. May be served with tomato slices and watercress sprig. Serves 4.

RECIPES

Carrot-Yogurt Salad
1 pound carrots, coarsely shredded
2 medium apples, grated
1 cup yogurt
1 tablespoon honey (optional)
juice from one lemon
salt, pepper
1 tablespoon sesame seeds (optional)
1/4 cup sunflower seeds, almonds, cashews (optional)
1/2 cup celery, finely minced (optional)
1/2 cup pineapple (optional)

Combine ingredients. Chill. Serves 4.

Cole Slaw
4 cups cabbage, finely shredded
2 carrots, grated
1/2 cup yogurt
1/2 cup mayonnaise
3 tablespoons vinegar
salt, pepper
1/2 cup green pepper, minced (optional)
1/2 cup red onion, thinly sliced (optional)

Combine ingredients. Chill several hours before serving. Serves 6.

* Fresh Fruit Salad*
1 small container yogurt or sour cream
1 apple
1 small package raisins
1 small package shredded coconut (optional)
1 banana
1 package ground nuts (optional)

Core and chop apple. Peel and slice banana. Mix all ingredients with sour cream or yogurt. Serves 2.

Fresh Veggie Salad
Fresh seasonal vegetables as available, such as: carrots, celery, cauliflower, broccoli,
    radishes, tomatoes
1 small head of lettuce (optional)
1 small bottle salad dressing of your choice

Chop vegetables and lettuce. Add dressing. Serves 1 or more, depending on quantities used.

Raw Vegetables
Use any crisp vegetables that can be eaten uncooked, such as: carrots, celery, broccoli, cauliflower, radishes

Wash. Remove inedible portions. Cut into easily manageable pieces.

Fresh Fruit
Use fresh seasonal fruit as available, such as: apples, grapes, melons

Wash. Remove rind or skins that would be difficult on the bike. Core, if appropriate, and cut into manageable pieces. Serve with cheese if desired.

Chilled Braised Asparagus with Vinaigrette
1 bunch asparagus (1 pound)
pan of ice water
vinaigrette (see next recipe)

Bring pot of salted water to a boil. Drop in asparagus spears. Cook until desired tenderness. Don't overcook. When tender, transfer to ice water. Let stand until cool, drain, and pat dry. Refrigerate for one day maximum. Add vinaigrette prior to serving. Serves 4.

Vinaigrette (for preceding recipe)
1 tablespoon Dijon-style mustard
4 tablespoons red wine vinegar
1 teaspoon granulated sugar
1/2 teaspoon salt
1/2 teaspoon ground black pepper
1/2 cup olive oil

RECIPES

Whisk mustard with vinegar, sugar, salt, and pepper. Add olive oil while continuing to whisk. Adjust seasonings to taste. Makes 1 cup.

Breads

Eric's Soft Pretzels
This makes a good fresh bread to eat with any of the above recipes.

1 package yeast
1 1/2 cups warm water
1 teaspoon salt
1 tablespoon sugar
4 cups flour
1 egg, beaten
coarse salt

Preheat oven to 425 degrees Fahrenheit. Measure warm water into large bowl. Add yeast. Add sugar, salt, and flour. Mix and knead. Form pretzels and place on a greased cookie sheet. Brush with egg and sprinkle with coarse salt. Bake 12 to 15 minutes. Serves 4 to 6 (depending on how far you've ridden).

Main Course Recipes
Though the first two recipes in this section are salads in concept, they are really light meals in their own right.

Larry's Artichoke Pasta Salad
This is only one of many pasta salad options. Vary this recipe using your imagination and the ingredients at hand.

4 ounces (about 1 cup) of medium-size pasta
1 jar (6 ounces) marinated artichoke hearts
1/4 pound small mushrooms
1 cup cherry tomatoes, halved
1 cup medium-size ripe pitted olives
1/2 teaspoon dry basil leaves
salt and pepper

Cook pasta, drain, rinse with cold water, and drain again. Mix pasta, artichokes with their liquid, mushrooms, tomatoes, olives, and basil in a large bowl. Toss gently. Refrigerate at least 4 hours. Season with salt and pepper to taste before serving. Serves 6.

Aunt Jan's High-Fiber Rice Salad
1/3 cup pine nuts
1/3 cup almonds
1/3 cup hazelnuts
1/3 cup pumpkin seeds
1 cup wild rice
1 cup brown rice
1/2 cup sliced green onions
1/2 cup celery
1/2 cup currants
1/2 cup nonfat yogurt
wine vinegar
olive oil
cayenne pepper (very important) and salt

Toast and then coarsely chop pine nuts, almonds, hazelnuts, and pumpkin seeds. Cook rice. Drain. Mix nuts, rice, onions, celery, and currants. Add wine vinegar, olive oil, cayenne pepper, and salt to the yogurt. Vary to your taste. Add yogurt dressing to rice mixture. Serve with pita bread. Serves 2 to 4.

Split Pea Parmesan Spread
1 cup cooked green split peas
2 tablespoons mayonnaise
2 tablespoons Parmesan cheese
2 tablespoons low-fat cottage cheese
1/2 teaspoon salt
1 teaspoon dry onion flakes

Mash split peas. Mix with other ingredients. Serve with pita bread. Serves 2.

Grilled Lemon Chicken
1 chicken, quartered or cut up
1 lemon, sliced
3 cloves garlic, crushed
1/2 cup oil, preferably olive oil
salt and pepper

105

The day before serving, marinate chicken in a shallow pan with lemon, oil, salt, and pepper. Grill over charcoal. May be served chilled or warm. Travels well. Serves 4.

Chicken, Cheese, and Chile Rolls á la Bruce
2 whole chicken breasts, halved
1/2 cup dry sherry
1/2 cups chicken broth
4 tablespoons prepared mustard
1/2 teaspoon garlic salt
pinch of dried sage, basil, and thyme
4 large slices jack cheese
4 strips canned peeled green chiles
4 frozen puff pastry shells
1 egg white, beaten
sesame seeds

Poach chicken breasts about 20 minutes in sherry and broth. Cool in poaching liquid for 30 minutes. Remove skin and bones, then refrigerate. Mix mustard and dry seasonings. Spread 1 tablespoon of mixture over each piece of chicken. Wrap a slice of cheese and chile around each piece. Let puff pastry stand at room temperature for 30 minutes. Roll each shell into an 8-inch circle (on lightly floured board). Place piece of wrapped chicken on shell, seam side down; bring up sides of pastry, overlap, moisten, and pinch. Place bundles, seam down, on ungreased cookie sheet. Brush with egg whites and sprinkle with seeds. Chill 30 minutes. Bake at 425 degrees F for 30 minutes or until brown and crisp. Cool on rack. Chill and serve. Makes 4.

Sandwich and Quick Meal Recipes

* Sandwiches*
Here are a few examples of suitable sandwiches for eating on the bike or at the picnic site. Be guided by your own imagination and the contents of your bread bin and refrigerator (or what's available along the way).

cream cheese on brown bread
cream cheese and cucumbers on crustless white bread
Swiss or Dutch cheese on French bread or brown bread
pastrami and Swiss on rye
roast beef on white bread

Cracker Sandwiches

Crackers or similar crisp breads can be used instead of bread for a large variety of crunchy sandwiches. Here are a few examples to get you started. Butter or margarine may be helpful in bonding the various ingredients together if they are hard cheeses, such as Swiss, Dutch, or American nonprocessed cheese. Use the bread of your choice with any of the following:

soft or hard cheese
cream cheese and jelly
processed cheese and jelly
salami and cheese

Cold Baked Potatoes

Baked potatoes may be the ultimate high-carbohydrate snack or main meal course. They are easy to make, particularly if you have a microwave, and are easy to carry. If you intend to eat on the bike, you may want to remove the peel beforehand. Make with any one of various toppings, limited only by your imagination. Unless eaten on the bike, the topping is best kept separate until it's time to eat.

Desserts

Arlene's Creamy Rice Pudding
1 cup rice
6 cups hot milk
1 teaspoon salt
2 tablespoons butter
2 teaspoons vanilla
2 teaspoons sugar

Place all ingredients in a pot that holds at least 8 cups. Cook over low heat (do not boil) for 1 hour. Remove and cool, then refrigerate. Excellent by itself or served with seasonal fruits. Serves 6.

French Apple and Bread Pudding
1/4 cup raisins or currants
1 large tart cooking apple
1/4 cup melted butter
4 beaten eggs
1 3/4 cups milk

107

1/2 cup heavy cream
1/2 cup sugar
1/2 teaspoon vanilla
2 cups unseasoned croutons or stale, dried bread
1/3 cup slivered almonds
1/8 cup brown sugar

Soak raisins or currants in small amount of water. Peel, core, and thinly slice apple. Cook apple slices in butter until translucent, then spoon into 1 1/2 quart casserole. In a separate bowl, beat eggs and then add milk, cream, sugar, and vanilla. Add croutons (cubed dried bread), currants, and remaining butter to casserole. Stir to mix with apples. Pour egg mixture into casserole and let stand 20 minutes. Sprinkle with nuts and brown sugar. Place casserole in large pan of water in oven. Bake at 350 degrees Fahrenheit for 40 minutes (or until knife comes out clean). Serves 6.

Apricot Cobbler
1 1/2 cups all-purpose flour
1/4 teaspoon salt
9 tablespoons unsalted butter
1/4 cup shortening
2 1/2 cups fresh ripe apricots
1 large tart apple: peeled, cored, and sliced
1 cup sugar

Preheat oven to 450 degrees Fahrenheit. In a food processor, process flour, salt, and 5 tablespoons of butter that has been previously frozen in small pieces. Add 1/4 cup ice water and process until dough begins to cling together (about 10 seconds). Drop apricots in boiling water for 10 seconds, then peel, pit, and cut into 1/2-inch-thick slices. Roll dough into a large circle and fit into a 1 1/2- to 2-quart baking dish. Place apricots into dough. Cover with sugar and dot with 4 tablespoons butter. Place in oven and reduce to 425 degrees Fahrenheit. Bake for 45 minutes. Serves 6 hungry bikers.

* Fresh Fruit and Cheese *
Any seasonal fruits, such as grapes, apples, pears, plums, figs, berries, and melons
Any kind of nonprocessed cheese

Wash fruit. Peel and core as appropriate. Combine fruit with cheese. May be prepared either at home or on site.

* Yogurt with Toppings*
1 container of yogurt (plain or flavor of choice)
fresh seasonal fruits as available (berries are great)
granola (packaged granola cereals work well here)
chopped nuts
toasted coconut

Mix yogurt with toppings of your choice.

* Berries on Shortcake*
1 package shortcakes (shortbread in Britain)
fresh berries as available (e.g., strawberries, raspberries, or blackberries)
1 can whipped cream

Shortcakes are particularly durable, and the berries can be added at the picnic site. The whipped cream really hits the spot after you've ridden a few hours.

Appendix A
Energy Requirements of Cycling

Expressed in terms of the number of Calories ingested

1. Level Surface (E_h = Energy required—horizontal)

$$P_w = v \times [3.509 + 0.2581 \times (v)^2]$$
$$P_c = P_w \div 4186.8$$
$$C_e = P_c \times T$$
$$C_i = C_e \div e = E_h$$

where:

P_w	=	power (watts)
v	=	velocity, or speed (m/sec)
P_c	=	power (Cal/sec)
T	=	time (sec)
C_e	=	Calories expended at the pedals
C_i	=	Calories ingested = E_h
e	=	efficiency of the human machine (approx. 25 percent)
E_h	=	energy required – horizontal

Assumptions:

75-kg rider
10-kg bike
level surface
no head wind

Definitions and conversion factors:

1 watt	=	1 joule/second
1 Cal	=	1,000 cal = 4,186.8 joules = 4,186.8 watts

2. Climbing Vertical Distance (E_v = Energy required—vertical)

$$W \quad = \quad F \times D$$
$$C_e \quad = \quad W \div CF$$
$$C_i \quad = \quad C_e \div e = E_v$$

where:

W	=	work (ft-lbs or kgm)
F	=	force from gravity (lbs or kg)
D	=	distance vertically (ft or m)
C_e	=	Calories expended at the pedals
CF	=	conversion factor of 3,097 or 418 (for American and international units, respectively)
C_i	=	Calories ingested = E_v
e	=	efficiency of the human machine (approx. 25 percent)
E_v	=	efficiency required – vertical

Definitions and conversion factors:

1 Cal	=	1,000 cal	=	4,184.8 joules
1 joule	=	74 ft-lbs	=	0.10 kgm
1 Cal	=	3,097 ft-lbs	=	418 kgm

3. Total Energy Requirements in Hilly Terrain

$$E_t \quad = \quad E_h + E_v$$

where:

E_t	=	Total energy requirements of cycling up a hill (in Calories ingested)
E_h	=	Energy requirements for horizontal distance covered (in Calories ingested)
E_v	=	Energy requirements for vertical distance climbed (in Calories ingested)

ENERGY REQUIREMENTS OF CYCLING

Example:

A 165-pound cyclist (75 kilograms) rides a 10-mile hilly route at an average speed of 15 miles per hour (6.7 meters per second). During the ride, he climbs 1,500 feet (457 meters). His bicycle weighs 22 pounds (10 kilograms). How many Calories will he need to eat to replace the energy expended?

$$P_w \quad = \quad 6.7\,[3.509 + 0.2581\,(6.7)^2]$$
$$= \quad 6.7\,[3.509 + 11.586]$$
$$= \quad 101 \text{ watts}$$
$$P_c \quad = \quad 101 \div 4,186.8 = 0.024 \text{ Cal/sec}$$
$$T \quad = \quad 10 \div 15 = 0.66 \text{ hr}$$
$$= \quad 0.66 \times 3,600$$
$$= \quad 2,376 \text{ sec}$$
$$C_e \quad = \quad 0.024 \times 2,376 = 57 \text{ Cal } 0.024 \times 2,376$$
$$C_i \quad = \quad 57 \text{ Cal} \div 0.25 = 228 \text{ Cal} = E_h$$
$$W \quad = \quad 85 \text{ kg} \times 457 \text{ m}$$
$$= \quad 38,845 \text{ kgm}$$
$$Ce \quad = \quad 38,845 \div 418 = 92 \text{ Cal}$$
$$C_i \quad = \quad 92 \div 0.25 = 371 \text{ Cal} = E_v$$
$$E_t \quad = \quad E_h + E_v$$
$$= \quad 228 \text{ Cal} + 371 \text{ Cal}$$
$$= \quad 599 \text{ Cal needed to replace those expended}$$

If one is a purist, 50 Cal/hour need to be added for basal metabolism.

Since this ride took 2/3 of an hour, the correct approximation is 599 + (2/3 x 50) = 632 Calories.

Appendix B
International Units

Scientific measurements can be expressed in several ways. English units (pound, inch) are still in common use in the United States. The rest of the world, including Great Britain, uses the International System of Units (SI Units). The latter is based on the metric system (kilogram, centimeter) and is used in most scientific texts.

Conversion Table

1 inch	=	2.54 centimeters
1 foot	=	0.305 meters
	=	30.5 cm
1 mile	=	1,609 m
	=	1.609 km
1 mph	=	1.609 km/hr
	=	0.445 m/sec
1 ounce	=	28.35 grams
1 pound	=	454 grams (mass)
	=	4.5 N(Newton) (force)
1 quart	=	947 cubic centimeters
	=	0.947 liter
1 watt	=	1 joule/sec
	=	0.014 Kilocalories/min
	=	0.014 Cal/min
1 joule	=	0.74 ft-lb
	=	1 Nm (corresponding to approximately 0.1 kgm under normal sea-level gravitational effects)
1 Calorie	=	3,097 ft-lbs
	=	1 kcal
	=	1,000 cal
	=	418 kgm
	=	4,184.6 joules (J)
	=	4.18 kilojoules (kJ)

Glossary

absolute work:
The actual number of Calories expended to accomplish a task. It is the same for all individuals and is not affected by the level of conditioning.

adenosine diphosphate (ADP):
A coenzyme that acts as an intermediate carrier in cellular metabolism. It is transformed into ATP (see below) by the addition of a phosphate group.

adenosine triphosphate (ATP):
An organic compound acting as a carrier for intermediary energy storage during cellular metabolism. It is the last chemical compound formed in the transfer of food energy into mechanical work.

aerobic metabolism:
Cellular energy release carried out in the presence of oxygen.

anaerobic metabolism:
Cellular energy release carried out without oxygen

basal metabolic rate (BMR):
The heat production (energy consumption) of an individual at the lowest level of cellular activity (metabolism) in the waking state.

bonk:
A descriptive term identifying that point at which liver glycogen is depleted and maximum energy output cannot be maintained. It can be delayed or reversed by eating carbohydrates.

caloric replacement:
The number of Calories that must be eaten to replace those required to carry out a certain amount of work.

calorie:
The old scientific unit of energy (superseded by the joule; see below). It is the energy required to raise the temperature of 1 gram of water 1 degree Centigrade.

Calorie:
A unit of energy equal to 1,000 calories. This is the unit used when referring to the energy content of foods as well as to the production and utilization of energy in humans.

carbohydrate:
An organic compound containing carbon, hydrogen, and oxygen. It is a basic source of energy for the cell and yields 4.1 Calories per gram.

cardiac output:
The rate at which blood is pumped by the heart, usually expressed in liters per minute.

century ride:
A bicycle ride of 100 miles. There can also be a "metric" century of 100 kilometers.

chyme:
The semifluid mass of partly digested food passed from the stomach into the duodenum.

complex carbohydrate:
An organic molecule composed of at least two simple (single) carbohydrate molecules.

concentration:
The quantity of any substance in a defined volume of a solution or mixture.

disaccharide:
A carbohydrate consisting of two molecules.

diuretic:
A compound that promotes water excretion by the kidneys.

GLOSSARY

efficiency:
The ratio of work output to energy input.

energy:
The capacity for doing work.

essential:
Necessary. In the context of nutrition, this refers to basic food elements (fats and amino acids) that cannot be synthesized by the body. These substances are each necessary for cellular metabolism and existence, making them essential components of the diet.

exhaustion:
The point at which the athlete cannot maintain an initial level of activity, even with an adequate blood glucose supply. Related to a change in the muscle itself—not the source of energy.

fatigue:
The point at which the body's glucose stores are depleted and all energy is derived from fat metabolism. It can be reversed with oral glucose supplements.

fatty acid (FA):
One of the molecules making up a triglyceride, the basic component of fatty tissue, and an essential intermediary in fat metabolism.

fluid deficit:
The difference between the body's ideal water content and its actual water content (usually after exercise).

fructose:
Fruit sugar. Important, as it can be metabolized to glycogen without insulin.

gluconeogenesis:
The production of glucose, a carbohydrate, from either fat or protein. It is often an intermediate step in energy production from these materials.

glucose:
The monosaccharide that is the most important carbohydrate in cellular metabolism.

glycogen:
The form in which carbohydrates are stored in the body. When needed, it is converted in the tissues into glucose.

hitting the wall:
A descriptive term identifying that point at which both liver and muscle glycogen have been depleted and maximum energy output cannot be maintained. It can be delayed by eating carbohydrates while exercising but cannot be reversed once it occurs.

international units:
See SI units.

joule:
The scientific unit of energy—see the conversion table in appendix B for the equivalent in calories and Calories.

lactic acid:
One of the by-products of anaerobic metabolism. It has a negative effect on muscle functioning and, in this way, limits athletic performance.

maximal oxygen consumption (VO2max):
The maximum amount (volume) of oxygen that an individual can consume in a set period of time (liters per minute). It can also be expressed per kilogram of body weight (ml/kg/min). It is a reflection of the upper limit of aerobic metabolism and is a product of the maximal cardiac output and maximal arterial-venous oxygen difference.

maximum heart rate (MHR):
The maximum attainable heart rate for an individual. It decreases with age and can be estimated using the formula: MHR = 220 − (age in years).

metabolism:
The biochemical cellular functions involved in energy production.

minerals:
Inorganic elements or compounds that are essential constituents of all cells.

GLOSSARY

mitochondria:
The component of the cell where glucose, fat, or protein are oxidized to release energy for cell activities.

monosaccharide:
A carbohydrate consisting of a single molecule.

osmotic activity:
Relating to the concentration (number of molecules in a given volume) of a solution.

oxidation:
Literally, the chemical combination with oxygen, releasing energy in the process.

oxygen consumption (VO2):
The total volume of oxygen consumed by the cells of the body over a given period of time in carrying out the basic metabolic functions.

oxygen debt:
The amount of oxygen required for the removal of the lactic acid and other metabolic products that accumulate during anaerobic metabolism.

paceline:
Several cyclists drafting (following closely) one another in a line to minimize energy needs and improve the performance of the group.

placebo:
An inactive compound given for suggestive effect.

polymer:
A substance made up of a chain of similar units. In the context of this text, it refers to a chain of simple glucose molecules.

power:
The rate at which work is done. For example, if an 80-kilogram bicycle and rider are raised 3 meters in 1 minute, power is expressed as 240 kilogram-meters per minute (kgm/h).

relative work rate:
The percentage of a person's VO2max required to accomplish a task. Even though the absolute work is the same for all riders, the relative work rate can vary from individual to individual, depending on the level of conditioning.

second wind:
The phenomenon of easing of effort for any given level of exercise which occurs after warming up. It is thought to relate, in some degree, to a shift from carbohydrate toward fat metabolism in the cells.

SI units (international units):
The international system of units (as opposed to the English system) based on the metric system. In nutritional literature, the English system remains widely accepted in the United States.

trace element:
Any mineral supplied by food that is only present in the body in a minute concentration.

triglyceride:
The basic molecule of fat (adipose) tissue. Triglycerides contain 9.3 Calories per gram.

urea:
The end product of protein metabolism in humans, which is excreted.

VO2max:
See maximal oxygen consumption.

work:
The application of a force over a (vertical) distance. For example, moving 80 kilograms up over a distance of 2 meters equals 160 kilogram-meters (kgm) of work.

Bibliography

Anderson, J., and B. L. Becker. "Carbohydrate Power." *Rx Being Well* (Sept./Oct. 1987): 41–45.

Askew, E. W. "Role of Fat Metabolism in Exercise." *Clinics in Sports Medicine* 3 (July 1984): 605–621.

Brouns, F., W. H. M. Saris, E. Beckers, H. Adlercreutz, G. J. van der Vusse, H. A. Kreizer, H. Kuipers, P. Menheere, A. J. M. Wagenmakers, and F. ten Hoor. "Metabolic Changes Induced by Sustained Exhaustive Cycling and Diet Manipulation." *Int. J. Sports Med.* 10 (1989): 49–S62.

Brouns, F., W. H. M. Saris, J. Stroecken, E. Beckers, R. Thijssen, N. J. Reher, and F. ten Hoor. "A Controlled Tour de France Simulation Study: Part 1 and Part 2." *Int. J. Sports Med.* 10 (1989): S32–S48.

Burke, E., H. R. Perez, and P. Hodges. *Inside the Cyclist.* Battleboro: Velo News, 1986.

Casal, D. C., and A. S. Leon. "Metabolic Effects of Caffeine on Submaximal Exercise Performance in Marathoners." *Med. Sci. Sports Exer.* 14 (1982): 176

Coggan, A. R., and E. F. Coyle. "Reversal of Fatigue during Prolonged Exercise by Carbohydrate Infusion or Ingestion." *J. Appl. Physiol.* 63 (1987): 2388–2395.

Costill, D. L. "Carbohydrates for Exercise: Dietary Demands for Optimal Performance." *Int. J. Sports Med.* 9 (1988): 1–18.

——. "Water and Electrolyte Requirements during Exercise." *Clinics in Sports Medicine* 3 (July 1984): 639–648.

Costill, D. L., W. M. Sherman, W. J. Fink et al. "The Role of Dietary Carbohydrates in Muscle Glycogen Resynthesis after Strenuous Running." *Amer. J. Clin. Nutr.* 34 (1981): 1831–1836.

Coyle, E. F. "Ergogenic Aids." *Clinics in Sports Medicine* 3 (July 1984): 731–742.

——. personal communication.

Coyle, E. F., A. R. Coggan, M. K. Hemmert et al. "Muscle Glycogen Utilization during Prolonged Strenuous Exercise When Fed Carbohydrate." *J. Appl. Physiol.* 61 (1986): 165–172.

Coyle, E. F., A. R. Coggan, M. K. Hemmert, R. C. Lowe, and T. J. Walters. "Substrate Usage during Prolonged Exercise Following a Pre-exercise Meal." *J. Appl. Physiol.* 59 (1985): 429–433.

Coyle, E. F., A. R. Coggan, M. K. Hopper, and T. J. Walters. "Determinants of Endurance in Well Trained Cyclists." *J. Appl. Physiol.* 64 (1988): 2622–2630.

Coyle, E. F., J. M. Hagberg, B. F. Hurley, W. H. Martin, A. A. Ehsani, and J. O. Holloszy. "Carbohydrate Feeding during Prolonged Strenuous Exercise Can Delay Fatigue." *J. Appl. Physiol.* 55 (1983): 230–235.

Dohm, G. L. "Protein Nutrition for the Athlete." *Clinics in Sports Medicine* 3 (July 1984): 595–604.

Dohm, G. L., R. T. Beeker, R. G. Israel, and E. B. Tapscott. "Metabolic Responses to Exercise after Fasting." *J. Appl. Physiol.* 61 (1986): 1363–1368.

Elliot, D. L., and L. Goldberg. "Nutrition and Exercise." *Med. Clin. N. Amer.* 69 (1985): 71–82.

"Exercise Slows GI Transit." *Gastroenterology Observer* 6 (1987): 7.

Faria, I. E. "Applied Physiology of Cycling." *Sports Medicine* 1 (1984): 187–204.

Gollnick, P. D., and H. Matoba. "Role of Carbohydrate in Exercise." *Clinics in Sports Medicine* 3 (July 1984): 583–593.

Gwinup, Dr., Divn. of Endocrinology and Metabolism, UC Irvine Med. Ctr. As presented at 37th Annual Obesity and Assoc. Cond. Symposium.

Hargreaves, M., D. L. Costill, A. Coggan, I. Nishibata, and W. J. Fink. "Carbohydrate Feedings and Exercise Performance." *Med. Sci. Sports Exer.* 15 (1983): 129.

Hecker, A. L. "Nutritional Conditioning." *Clinics in Sports Medicine* 3 (July 1984): 567–582.

Higdon, H. "Breakfast (Lunch and Dinner) of Champions." *Hippocrates* 2 (1988): 44–58.

Holloszy, J. O., M. J. Rennie, R. C. Hickson et al. "Physiologic Consequences of the Biochemical Adaptions to Endurance Exercise." *Ann. NY Acad. Sci.* 301 (1977): 440–450.

Ivy, J. L. "Effect of Amount of a Carbohydrate Supplement on a Rapid Glycogen Resynthesis Post Exercise." *J. Appl. Physiol.* 1988: In Press.

Ivy, J. L., D. L. Costill, J. W. Fink, and R. W. Lower. "Influence of Caffeine and Carbohydrate Feedings on Endurance Performance." *Med. and Science in Sports* 11 (1979): 6–11.

Ivy, J. L., A. L. Katz., C. L. Cutler et al. "Muscle Glycogen Synthesis after Exercise: Effect of Time of Carbohydrate Ingestion." *J. Appl. Physiol.* 64 (1988): 1480–1485.

Karlsson, J., and B. Saltin. "Diet, Muscle Glycogen, and Endurance Performance." *J. Appl. Physiol.* 31 (1971): 203–206.

King, A. C., B. Frey-Hewitt, D. M. Dreon, and P. D. Wood. "Diet versus Exercise in Weight Maintenance." *Arch. Int. Med.* 142 (1989): 2741–2746.

BIBLIOGRAPHY

Larson, E. B., and R. A. Bruce. "Editorial: Exercise and Aging." *Ann. of Int. Med* 105 (Nov. 1986): 783–785.

Locksley, R. "Fuel Utilization in Marathons: Implications for Performance." *West. J. Med.* 133 (1980): 493–502.

Loy, S. F., R. K. Conlee, W. W. Winder, A. G. Nelson, D. A. Arnall, and A. G. Fisher. "Effects of 24-Hour Fast on Cycling Endurance Time at Two Different Intensities." *J. Appl. Physiol.* 61 (1986): 654–659.

McCole, S. D., K. Claney, J. Conte et al. "Energy Expenditure during Bicycling." *J. Appl. Physiol.* 68 (1990): 748–753.

Merkin, G. "Eating for Competition." *Seminars in Adolescent Medicine* 3 (1987): 177–183.

Meyers, F., and R. S. Fischer. "A Rational Approach to Gastric Emptying Disorders." *International Medicine* 9 (1988): 112–122.

Morella, J. J., and R. J. Turchetti. *Nutrition and the Athlete.* Van Nostrand Reinhold Company, 1982.

Neufer, P. D., D. L. Costill, M. G. Flynn, J. P. Kirwan, J. B. Mitchell, and J. Houmard. "Improvements in Exercise Performance: Effects of Carbohydrate Feedings and Diet." *J. Appl. Physiol.* 62 (1987): 983–988.

O'Toole, M. L., P. S. Douglas, W. D. B. Hiller. "Applied Physiology of a Triathlon." *Sports Medicine* 8 (1989): 201–225.

Pena, N. "Legal Performance Enhancers." *Bicycling* 28 (July 1987): 30–34.

———. "What Does This Man Know That You Don't?" *Bicycling* 19 (1988): 73–77.

Pierce, E. F., A. Weltman, R. L. Seip, and D. Snead. "Effects of Training Specificity on the Lactate Threshold and VO2 Peak." *Int. J. Sports Med.* 11 (1990): 267–272.

"Position of the American Dietetic Association: Nutrition for Physical Fitness and Athletic Performance for Adults." *J. Am. Dietetic Assoc.* 87 (1987): 933–939.

Powers, S. K., R. J. Byrd, R. Tulley, and T. Calender. "Effects of Caffeine Ingestion on Metabolism and Performance during Graded Exercise." *Med. Sci. Sports Exer.* 14 (1982): 176.

Pritikin, N. *Diet for Runners.* New York: Simon and Schuster, 1982.

Recommended Dietary Allowances. National Academy of Sciences, 1980.

Roedde, S., J. D. MacDougall, J. R. Sutton, and H. J. Green. "Supercompensation of Muscle Glycogen in Trained and Untrained Subjects." *Canad. J. Appl. Sports Sciences* 11 (1986): 42–46.

Saris, W. H. M., M. A. van Erp-Baart, F. Brouns, K. R. Westerterp, and F. ten Hoor. "Study on Food Intake and Energy Expenditure during Extreme Sustained Exercise: The Tour de France." *Int. J. Sports Med.* 10 (1989): S26–S31.

Schneider, D. A., K. A. LaCroix, G. R. Atkinson, P. J. Troped, and J. Pollack. "Ventilatory Threshold and Maximal Oxygen Uptake during Cycling and Running in Triathletes." *Med. Sci. Sports Exer.* 22 (1990): 257–264.

Schoene, R. B. "Nutrition for Ultra-endurance: Several Hours to Several Months." *Clinics in Sports Medicine* 3 (July 1984): 679–692.

Sherman, W. M., G. Brodowicz., D. A. Wright, W. K. Allen, J. Simonsen, and A. Dernbach. "Effects of 4-Hour Pre-exercise Carbohydrate Feedings on Cycling Performance." *Med. Sci. Sports. Exer.* 21 (1989): 598–604.

Simons-Morton, B. G., R. R. Pate, and D. G. Simons-Morton. "Prescribing Physical Activity to Prevent Disease." *Postgraduate Medicine* 83 (1988): 165–176.

Smith, N. J. "Weight Control in the Athlete." *Clinics in Sports Medicine* 3 (July 1984): 693–704.

Stewart, I., L. McNaughton, P. Davies, and S. Tristan. "Phosphate Loading and the Effects on VO2max in Trained Cyclists." *Research Quarterly for Exercise and Sport* 61 (1990): 80–84.

White, J., and M. A. Ford. "The Hydration and Electrolyte Maintenance Properties of an Experimental Sports Drink." *Brit. J. Sports Medicine* 17 (1983): 51–58.

White, J. A., C. Ward, and H. Nelson. "Ergogenic Demands of a 24-Hour Cycling Event." *Brit. J. Sports Medicine* 18 (1984): 165–171.

Whitney, E. N. *Nutrition—Concepts and Controversies.* West Publishing Company, 1982.

Whitt, F. R., and D. G. Wilson. *Bicycling Science.* Cambridge: MIT Press, 1982.

Williams, M. H. "Vitamin and Mineral Supplements to Athletes: Do They Help?" *Clinics in Sports Medicine* 3 (July 1984): 623–637.

Wilmore, J. H., and B. J. Freund. "Nutritional Enhancement of Athletic Performance." *Current Concepts in Nutrition* 15 (1986): 67–97.

Young, V. R. "Protein and Amino Acid Metabolism in Relation to Physical Exercise." *Current Concepts in Nutrition* 15 (1986): 9–32.

Zahradnik, F. "Sports Drinks." *Bicycling* 28 (September 1987): 46–50.

Zanecosky, A. "Nutrition for Athletes." *Clinics in Podiatric Medicine and Surgery* 3 (1986): 623–630.

Index